THE CHICKEN COOKBOOK

THE CHICKEN COOKBOOK

WENDY VEALE

GALLERY BOOKS
An Imprint of W. H. Smith Publishers Inc.

A QUINTET BOOK

This edition first published in the United States
in 1990 by Gallery Books,
an imprint of W.H. Smith Publishers, Inc.,
112 Madison Avenue, New York 10016

Gallery books are available for bulk purchase for sales
promotion and premium use. For details write or
telephone the Manager of Special Sales, W.H. Smith
Publishers, Inc., 112 Madison Avenue, New York,
New York 10016. (212) 532-6600.

ISBN 0-8317-1763-7

CREATIVE DIRECTOR: Peter Bridgewater
ART DIRECTOR: Ian Hunt
DESIGNER: Sally McKay
ARTWORK: Danny McBride
ILLUSTRATIONS BY: Bee Willey
PHOTOGRAPHY: Ian Howes
EDITOR: Barbara Fuller

Typeset in Great Britain by
Central Southern Typesetters, Eastbourne
Manufactured in Hong Kong by
Regent Publishing Services Limited
Printed in Hong Kong by
Leefung Asco Printers Limited

This cookery book will, I hope, be an invaluable addition to
your collection. It has been written with the healthy diet in
mind, but without sacrificing too many of the enjoyable
ingredients.

CONTENTS

INTRODUCTION

CHOOSING THE RIGHT CHICKEN

Chicken rearing and production will determine the flavour and texture of the bird; so will its age. A 'free range' chicken, for example, will have more taste and will need a milder accompaniment than a factory-farmed bird, though it probably won't be as tender. Young birds are ideal for grilling or sautéing – a quick method of sealing in the mild, subtle flavour whilst retaining succulence. Older birds become tough, and require long, slow cooking to tenderize the muscle fibres.

POUSSINS (CORNISH GAME HENS)
These are baby chickens of 4 to 6 weeks old and weighing about 0.5 kg (1 lb). There is not a great deal of flavour in them, and they are best marinaded and then grilled (broiled). A poussin (Cornish game hen) usually serves one person and is available fresh or frozen.

DOUBLE POUSSIN
A chicken weighing around 1 kg (2 to 2¼ lb). Again, they are best grilled (broiled) or spit-roasted.

SPRING CHICKEN
A 12 to 14-week-old chicken averaging 1.1 kg (2½ lb). Roast, spit-roast, grill (broil) or sauté.

BROILERS
A 2 to 4-month-old bird, weighing 1.1 to 1.5 kg (2½ to 3½ lb). One of the most widely sold birds, these are tender but not the most tasty. Grill (broil) or sauté for best results, or roast with a well-flavoured stuffing.

ROASTING CHICKENS
These chickens are 8 to 9 months old and have developed to produce a good flavour. Weighing 1.75 to 2.25 kg (4 to 5 lb), this bird is perfect for roasting and casseroling.

BOILING FOWL
This chicken is usually 12 months old or more and weighs 2.75 to 3.5 kg (6 to 8 lb). It is most suitable for slow casserole cooking or soup and stock making, and cooks well in a pressure cooker. It has a rich flavour and is particularly meaty. Smaller, less plump birds, usually weighing 1.1 to 1.5 kg (2½ to 3½ lb) can also be classified as boiling fowl.

CAPON
This is a cockerel which has been injected with hormone capsules to neuter (caponize) it. It is specially bred to produce a good, meaty roast, and weighs 2.25 to 3.5 kg (5 to 8 lb). Capons are usually sold at Christmas, but have a very small share in the market.

POULARDE
This is a hen which has been neutered to increase its size. As with the capon, a good-sized roaster will be produced, weighing 1.75 kg (4 lb) or over.

CORN-FED CHICKENS
These chickens are specially reared on a diet of maize grains which gives the bird a distinct yellow hue and a good flavour. They are available fresh and are categorized as broilers.

BUYING FRESH CHICKEN
When selecting and buying fresh oven-ready chickens, choose a reputable poulterer, butcher or retailer who has a good, high-quality supplier, a frequent turnover and the time to advise.

Look for a bird with a healthy, pinkish hue, check that it is free from bruising or any other damage, and if it is a roasting bird, the breastbone should be soft and flexible, and the breast plump.

Always check the sell-by date carefully.

STORAGE
FROZEN CHICKENS
When storing a frozen whole chicken, or frozen chicken portions, always follow the instructions on the pack.

Ready-frozen poultry should be transported home as quickly as possible, preferably in an insulated coolbag, and then stored in the home freezer for the recommended time:

RECOMMENDED FREEZER STORAGE PERIODS	
Frozen whole chicken	3 months
Frozen chicken portions	3 months
Cooked chicken	2 months
Giblets	3 months
Boiling Fowl	9 months

FRESH CHICKENS
Fresh chickens, whole or portioned, often carry storage instructions if bought from a large retailer.

If they are already wrapped in packs, the seal should be broken to allow air to circulate, and the chicken to 'breathe'. Otherwise remove wrapping, and giblets if included, and place the chicken on a plate. Cover loosely and put in the lowest (coolest) part of the refrigerator. The chicken will keep for several days.

Ready-cooked chickens should be refrigerated as soon as possible and eaten within 2 to 3 days.

THAWING FROZEN CHICKENS
Frozen chickens must be thoroughly defrosted prior to cooking. If not, and the bird is cooked while still partially frozen, it may not cook all the way through in the recommended time and food poisoning can occur. Therefore, forward planning is important. Ideally a chicken should be thawed in the refrigerator, ensuring that it stays fresh.

The thawing times below are recommended by the British Chicken Information Service given opposite.

Once the bird is defrosted, check to see that there are no ice crystals in the cavity, and that the legs and thighs are pliable. Always ensure that the defrosting bird is on a plate or drip tray and placed at the bottom of the fridge. Otherwise, any uncooked juices from the chicken which drip onto other foods can pass on bacteria and cause food spoilage.

This rule applies to any fresh meat or poultry.

Weight	Thawing at Room Temperature (16°C/65°F)	Thawing in Refrigerator (4°C/39°F)
1 kg (2 lb)	8 hours	28 hours
1.25 kg (3 lb)	9 hours	32 hours
1.75 kg (4 lb)	14 hours	50 hours
3 kg (7 lb)	16 hours	56 hours

METHODS OF COOKING CHICKEN

There are four principal methods of cooking whole and portioned chickens, and, as highlighted opposite , the type and age of the chicken will have a great bearing on the most suitable method.

Let's take a look at these principal methods, followed by some alternative and less familiar or obvious cooking methods.

ROASTING

Traditionalists still find great comfort in, and enjoy the ritual of, a roast dinner. It is home cooking at its best and, more often than not, is an occasion shared with a number of family and friends.

Today, roasts are prepared in the oven – the bird or joint is cooked in a current of air by dry (or radiant) heat. An alternative method is the rôtisserie, which is the modern equivalent of true roasting in Medieval Europe. Then, the bird was impaled on a spit and roasted over or in front of an open fire (in fact, true roasting is more like grilling as we know it).

Roasting is only suitable for tender cuts of meat or poultry, as the meat fibres and tissues will shrink and toughen slightly in the initial high temperatures required to seal the outside surfaces. This 'sealing' ensures that flavoursome juices will be kept in the bird, providing a moister, full-flavoured roast.

Because of its very nature, chicken does not contain a high proportion of fatty tissues and the bird can dry out very quickly during roasting. At one time 'larding' the chicken was commonplace. This was done by threading strips of fat (usually bacon) through the flesh. Now, 'barding' is recommended – a much simpler method, overlapping strips of fatty bacon along the breast of the chicken. During cooking, the bacon will 'baste' the chicken and protect it from drying out. The bacon is removed to one side half an hour before the end of cooking to allow the

chicken skin to brown and crispen. (And the bacon is not wasted – it's a delicious accompaniment to the bird.)

Mass-produced chickens will benefit from a forcemeat or stuffing. Tucked inside the body cavity, under the breast skin, or both, a stuffing will add both moisture and flavour to the chicken (see Traditional Accompaniments).

The method of roasting a chicken is given on page 77 . Meanwhile, below is a guide to the oven temperature and cooking times required for the perfect roast chicken.

Foil will help to retain the bird's natural juices, and also cuts down on the need for basting. However, as the chart shows, additional cooking time is required.

Roasting Bags work well with chicken. Not only do they help keep the oven clean, but they also self-baste and brown the chicken. They are available in a variety of sizes. It is important to pierce the bag, or cut away a corner, to allow the steam to escape. This not only ensures that the chicken will brown and crispen, but also prevents the bag from exploding!

Basting. As well as barding the chicken breasts with fatty bacon, brushing the chicken with a little oil or melted butter before roasting helps to protect the flesh and crispen the skin. Baste the chicken regularly – every 15 to 20 minutes or so – to keep it moist.

IS THE CHICKEN COOKED?

Insert a thin skewer into the thickest part of the thigh. If the juices run out clear, then the bird is cooked. Alternatively, tip the chicken up and examine the juices escaping from the body cavity. Again, the should be clear.

The leg is also a good indicator: the meat tends to shrink from the end of the drumstick and the leg, when tugged gently away from the body, will 'give'.

RELAXING

Once any joint or whole bird is cooked, it needs some 'standing time' on a hot dish in a warm place. This allows for all the juices which, during cooking, have drawn up to the surface of the chicken to redistribute back into the flesh. Allow 10 to 15 minutes for this. It is well worthwhile, producing a better, more succulent texture and making carving easier.

2 POT ROASTING, BRAISING OR CASSEROLING

Pot Roasting is the equivalent of the French method of braising.

Chicken Weight	Cooking Time	Oven Temp	Stuffed Bird	Foil Wrapped Bird
1.5 kg and under (3½ lb)	20 mins per 500 g/lb + 20 mins extra	190°C/375°F/Gas 5	Add 20–25 mins extra to the overall time	Add 15 mins extra to the overall time. Pull back the foil for last 20 mins. cooking time to allow chicken to brown.
1.75 kg–2.75 kg (4–6 lb)	25 mins per 500 g/lb + 25 mins extra	170°C/325°F/Gas 3	Add 20–25 mins extra to the overall time	Add 15 mins extra to the overall time. Pull back the foil for last 20 mins. cooking time to allow chicken to brown.

It is a combination of a type of stew and roast. Whereas a traditional roast can take up time and attention, a pot roast, or braise, allows you to use older, tougher joints and birds which require longer, slower methods of cooking, and leave you free to attend to other things. A French braising pan or a cast-iron casserole which can be used both over direct heat and in the oven is ideal. These need a tight-fitting lid, otherwise flavouring juices will evaporate and escape.

The principle of pot roasting or braising is to first seal the chicken over a direct heat and then add some herbs, vegetables and just enough stock or wine to cover the vegetables. The liquid will baste and keep the chicken moist, and can then be used in an accompanying sauce. Once the lid is fitted on and the pot roast is transferred to a slow oven (170°C/325°F/Gas 3), the chicken will cook in a moist, steamy atmosphere. The lid may be removed, and the heat increased for a short time towards the end of the cooking period to brown and roast the surface of the chicken.

Cooking time is about 25 per cent longer than roasting, but it is well worth it, as the bird will be tender and very succulent.

Casseroling is a long, slow method of cooking chicken and meats in the oven (not to be confused with stewing which takes place on top of the cooker). Vegetables, herbs and stock or wine are added to the sealed whole chicken, or portions, and it is then given just enough heat to simmer the liquid gently for as long as is required to tenderize the tougher older bird. A well-fitting lid, again, is important to retain the juices.

3 SAUTÉING, SHALLOW & DEEP FAT FRYING

Fried foods have, over the past few years, become taboo. Associations with saturated fats, cholesterol and heart problems have steered the majority of us away to more healthy methods of cooking.

However, there are some recipes which cannot, and indeed, should not avoid this integral method of cooking.

Sautéing is often required to seal and brown chicken portions before transferring them to a casserole dish. Sautéing is an excellent method of cooking chicken pieces; it keeps them tender and succulent, is an easy and quick method of cooking, and is the healthiest way of savouring 'fried' foods.

'Sauté' derives from the French verb 'sauter' – to jump. Although the flick of the wrist will not be required to continually toss the chicken (so making it jump), the portions will need to be turned frequently to maintain a golden brown colour and ensure even cooking. With the range of polyunsaturated fats now available, and good non-stick frying pans on the market, sautéed chicken can be included in a healthy eating plan.

The French may sauté, but the Chinese stir-fry in a wok!

Shallow Frying requires the chicken portion, first coated in seasoned flour or eggs and breadcrumbs, to be half submerged in 1.25 cm (½ in) hot oil or fat. The result is a crispy outer 'shell' concealing a moist and succulent chicken portion. The chicken will require turning half way through cooking. Take care not to over-crowd the pan, as this can not only cause the food to overlap and 'steam', but it also lowers the temperature causing the food to absorb unnecessary oil. Choose a polyunsaturated oil such as sunflower or corn oil to shallow fry in.

Deep Fat Frying. Deep fried chicken drumsticks, sizzling in golden oil, can be enough to tempt even the strictest of healthy food followers. A light, crisp batter, concealing a juicy chicken wing or perhaps the breadcrumbed Russian version concealing butter, garlicky juices of Chicken Kiev, are enough to cause the most dedicated and calorie-conscious amongst us to waiver. Once in a while we can cope with such indulgences – but it is best not to make a habit of it!

Deep-fried foods are fattening and often indigestible. The latter is due to the oil being too cool, either from overloading the pan with too much food, or underheating the oil. The protective batter or breadcrumb coating on the food will not instantly seal and, instead, absorbs the oil. The food becomes greasy and soggy, rather than crisp and appetising. On the other hand, if the oil is too hot, the 'shell' will brown too quickly and possibly burn on the outside before cooking the contents.

Careful cooking is required at a temperature of between 180 and 190°C (350–375°F), and don't forget the polyunsaturated oil. At least that will help ease the conscience a little.

4 GRILLING (BROILING) & BARBECUING

Grilling (broiling) is a very similar cooking method to roasting. The obvious difference, however, is that instead of surrounding the chicken with a dry, intense heat in an oven cavity, grilling radiates heat from one direction – above, or as in the case of a barbecue, below.

Grilling (broiling) is a delicious method of cooking the most tender, small chickens, poussins (Cornish game hens) and portions. It is a quick method, but requires constant attention, turning the chicken, sealing it on all sides and occasionally basting it.

Because the younger chicken may lack maturity, a marinade is an excellent way of adding flavour before cooking (see page 15). It can also be brushed on the bird as it grills, to prevent it from drying out.

Barbecuing. When cooking on a barbecue, sprigs of fresh herbs sprinkled on the coals will emit appetizing smells.

Having provided a brief resumé of the four main methods of cooking chicken, here are other suitable, although less used, methods of cooking.

1 THE CHICKEN BRICK

This is a very healthy and under-estimated method of cooking a whole roasting chicken. The chicken is placed in a clay chicken brick (which has previously been soaked in water for 25 minutes), and then simply placed in a preheated oven and cooked for the usual recommended times, but at a high temperature. Because the chicken will cook in its own juices, no added fats or basting is required; the chicken retains its own flavour and nutrients.

2 THE MICROWAVE OVEN

Chickens can be successfully defrosted and cooked in the microwave oven, and once the manufacturer's instructions have been carefully read, and the method mastered, the results are moist and tender. However, as with all alternative methods of cooking, a little practice will make perfect. The following chart shows the different cooking times determined by the power of the microwave oven.

Chicken	Quantity	Cooking Times		
		400W	500–600W	650–700W
Whole bird. Place breast side down in pierced roasting bag, using rack to keep meat clear of juices. Allow to stand for 15–20 minutes, wrapped in foil.	500 g (1 lb)	12	8	6
	1 kg (2 lb)	20	14	10
	1.5 kg (3 lb)	28	20	15
	1.75 kg (4 lb)	38	26	21
	2.25 kg (5 lb)	50	33	26
	2.7 kg (6 lb)	62	40	32
Chicken portion with bone*	2 portions	12	8	6
	4 portions	17	13	9
Chicken portion without bone (eg breast)**	2 portions	8	5	4
	4 portions	12	8	6

* Arrange in single layer with thinner end towards centre.
**Brush with oil or melted butter, turning over once during cooking.

3 PRESSURE COOKING
This is a quick and economical method of cooking chicken, but as with the microwave oven, models vary and instructions must be followed carefully.

4 STEAMING
Steaming is a quick, natural and healthy way of cooking and an excellent method of retaining nutrients and flavour. This moist method of cooking is ideal for chicken which does have a tendency to dry out easily. A 250 g (8 oz) breast will require 20 to 25 minutes, and a 250 g (8 oz) leg, 30 to 35 minutes.

5 ELECTRIC SLOW COOKING
Slow cookers are useful for the person with a hectic lifestyle. It allows long, slow cooking completely unattended. It is the same cooking method, in principle, as braising and casseroling, but sits on the worktop and is plugged in to an electrical power point. The long period of cooking in a moist atmosphere will tenderize the toughest of birds. A 1.5 kg (3½ lb) whole chicken will take 4 hours on the high setting to cook, but will sit quite happily for another hour without spoiling. Always refer to the manufacturer's instruction book before using.

6 POACHING
Poaching is carried out in 'shivering' as opposed to 'simmering' water (see Glossary page 94). Because of the low cooking temperature, true poaching is only applicable to fish and eggs.

However, for poultry, the water or stock is kept just under the boil, at a steady simmer. The results, though simple, are delicious. The chicken is moist and tender, any accompanying garden vegetables are full of flavour, and the resulting broth can be made into a wholesome soup or stock.

Henry IV of France declared 'I want there to be no peasant in my kingdom so poor that he cannot have a chicken in his pot every Sunday' – hence the famous 'poulet au pot'. (See page 79.)

PORTIONING, CARVING & JOINTING

PORTIONING
Depending on whether you are buying a chicken whole or already conveniently portioned, there can still be room for doubt over the quantity of meat to allow per person.

Chicken portions – part-boned or boneless breasts, legs, quarters, wings, thighs and drumsticks are one of the easiest options.

The size and number of portions to allow depends very much on the recipe involved, and your own appetite. And, of course, the size of the original chicken also has a great bearing. Here is an approximate guide:

Portion per person	Cooked plainly	Cooked in sauce or with other ingredients
Part-boned breast	175–250 g (6–8 oz)	125–175 g (4–6 oz)
Boneless breast	175 g (6 oz)	125 g (4 oz)–150 g (5 oz)
Chicken quarter	300–375 g (10–12 oz)	300 g (10 oz)
Chicken leg	250–300 g (8–10 oz)	200–250 g 7–8 oz)
Chicken thighs	3	2
Chicken wings	4–6	2–4
Chicken drumsticks	3	2
Cold cooked chicken meat	175 g (6 oz)	125 g (4 oz)

Allowances have been made for general wastage – skin, bones, etc.

For chickens to be cooked whole, there is a standard rule of thumb which works well and provides a certain amount of leeway.

For each person, allow 375 to 500 g (¾ to 1 lb). So, for example, a 1.1 to 1.25 kg (2½ to 3 lb) chicken will serve 2 to 3 people, a 1.75 to 2.25 kg (4 to 5 lb) chicken will serve 4 to 5 people, and so on.

CARVING A CHICKEN
Always allow the cooked chicken to 'stand' for 15 minutes before carving. Not only is the bird more succulent, but the flesh and juices have 'relaxed' and make carving easier.

If you don't have your own 'trencher' in the household do make sure you have a sturdy non-slip carving plate or board and a long sharp carving knife and fork. Carving poultry is simple if you follow these basic guidelines:

(i) Press the thigh down and away from the chicken body to reveal the leg joint. Secure the chicken with the fork and insert the knife between the body and leg to remove the leg. Separate the drumstick from the thigh to produce two leg portions (unless the bird is very small).

(ii) To remove the wing, take a line from the top of the wish-bone right down through the joint, to include a reasonable portion of breast meat.

(iii) Thinly slice the remaining breast.

(iv) Repeat with the other side of the bird. Don't forget to remove the 'oysters', two tiny meaty delicacies positioned in hollows on each side of the back.

JOINTING A CHICKEN

A little awesome at first, but certainly nothing to worry about. Nature provided the chicken with obvious incision lines – all you need is a sharp boning knife and a pair of poultry shears (good kitchen scissors or secateurs will do).

You may find a fresh chicken much easier to handle than a thawed 'frozen' chicken which may be more slippery.

This method provides 8 small portions.

(i) To remove the legs: stretch the leg outward as far as you can and cut through the natural line dividing the leg from the breast. Pull the thigh bone back at the bottom to reveal the joint. Cut through. Repeat with the other leg.

(ii) Turn the leg over, find the thin white line at the centre of the joint and cut through it. Repeat with the remaining leg. Now you have 4 portions.

(iii) To remove each breast: carefully cut down one side of the breastbone, scraping with the knife to remove the flesh from the bone, while carefully lifting the flesh away, taking the wing with it. Repeat on the other side.

(iv) Lay the breasts on a chopping board and cut each in half diagonally, so that the wing has a section of breast with it.

You now have 8 portions.

There are other methods of jointing a chicken, to produce anything from 4 to 10 portions.

If there are any bones remaining, use them to make stock.

Once this skill is acquired, it does not take long to joint a bird. However, if you are hesitant or in doubt, your friendly butcher should oblige.

NOTES ON THE RECIPES

Ingredients are given in American, metric and imperial measures. Use only one set of quantities, for any one recipe.

All spoon measurements are level unless specified.

Half a teaspoonful (½ tsp) = 2.5 ml
One teaspoonful (1 tsp) = 5 ml
One tablespoonful (1 tbsp) = 15 ml

WEIGHTS AND MEASURES

Metric	American/Imperial
15 g	½ oz
25 g	1 oz
125 g	4 oz
250 g	8 oz
375 g	12 oz
500 g	1 lb
750 g	1½ lb
1 kg	2 lb
1.25 kg	3 lb
1.75 kg	4 lb

VOLUME (liquid)

American	Metric	Imperial
¼ cup	60 ml	4 tbsp
	100 ml	3 fl oz
½ cup	125 ml	4 fl oz
	150 ml	5 fl oz/¼ pt
	200 ml	7 fl oz
1¼ cup	300 ml	10 fl oz/½ pt
1½ cup	375 ml	12 fl oz
2½ cup	600 ml	20 fl oz/1 pt
	750 ml	1¼ pt
	900 ml	1½ pt
	1.2 l	2 pt
	1.75 l	3 pt

OVEN TEMPERATURES

Ovens should be preheated to the temperature specified.

130 °C	250 °F	Gas ½
140 °C	275 °F	Gas 1
150 °C	300 °F	Gas 2
160 °C	325 °F	Gas 3
180 °C	350 °F	Gas 4
190 °C	375 °F	Gas 5
200 °C	400 °F	Gas 6
220 °C	425 °F	Gas 7

Eggs are standard size 3, ie medium, unless otherwise stated.

When fresh herbs are unavailable, use dried herbs but halve the quantity, unless otherwise indicated.

BASIC RECIPES

RAYMOND BLANC'S BROWN CHICKEN STOCK BROTH

A dark, brown chicken stock is used for the stronger flavoured, richer sauces and casseroles. Although this recipe may seem a great deal of effort for so small a quantity of juices, it is well worth it.

- ☐ In a large roasting pan, heat the vegetable oil until smoking, then brown the chicken wings or carcasses for 8 to 10 minutes, stirring occasionally with a wooden spoon.
- ☐ In a small bowl mix the peppercorns, onion, garlic, thyme and bayleaf, then add to the chicken and cook for a further 5 minutes. Transfer to the oven and cook for 20 minutes or until a rich brown.
- ☐ Meanwhile brush the tomatoes with a little vegetable oil and cook them in the oven for 10 minutes until brown. Add to the chicken wings or carcass. Transfer the roasting pan to the hob.
- ☐ Deglaze the roasting pan with 1 cup/200 ml/7 fl oz of the water, scraping up all the caramelized juices from the bottom of the pan. Add the remaining water, bring to the boil, and return to the hot oven for 20 minutes.
- ☐ Strain the juices into a small saucepan, bring to the boil, skim and reduce to about 2¼ cups/500 ml/18 fl oz tasty clear brown stock. Cool, then refrigerate.
- ☐ Remove any fat which has settled on the surface, seal with cling film (plastic wrap) and store until needed.

This stock can be made in advance and kept in the fridge for 1 week or in the freezer for 3 weeks.

VARIATIONS
CHICKEN DEMI-GLACE
Reduce the juices by half.

CHICKEN GLAZE
Reduce the juices to ⅓ cup/90 ml/6 tbsp to obtain a concentrated essence.

MAKES APPROX 2¼ CUPS/
500 ML/18 FL OZ

1.5 kg/3½ lb chicken wings or carcasses
⅓ cup/90 ml/6 tbsp vegetable oil
6 black peppercorns, crushed
1 medium onion, finely chopped
1 clove garlic, crushed (minced)
1 sprig thyme
½ bayleaf
4 medium tomatoes, halved
3¾ cups/900 ml/1 ½ pint water

Oven temperature: 230 °C/450 °F/Gas 8

**MAKES: 4 ½ CUPS/I LITRE/
I ¾ PINT STOCK**

*2 kg/4 ½ lb chicken wings or carcasses
(or a boiling chicken)
15 ml/I tbsp unsalted butter
white of I small leek, finely chopped
I small onion, finely chopped
I celery stalk, finely chopped
⅓ cup/100 g/3 ½ oz button mushrooms, sliced
I clove garlic, crushed (minced)
I sprig parsley, washed and shaken dry
I sprig thyme
½ fresh bayleaf
10 white peppercorns
scant cup/200 ml/7 fl oz dry white wine (optional)
4 ½ cups/I litre/I ¾ pt cold water*

RAYMOND BLANC'S LIGHT CHICKEN STOCK (BROTH)

A good clear stock is the very foundation of most soups, sauces and gravies, enhancing and enriching the flavours of many dishes.

Stocks can be stored in the freezer, so it is very worthwhile to take advantage of the opportunity to boil up the bones and carcasses of chickens, prepare a good stock and freeze it in small quantities until required.

☐ In a large pan, 'sweat' the chicken wings or carcass in the melted butter for 5 minutes without colouring. Add the chopped vegetables and crushed peppercorns and 'sweat' for a further 5 minutes.

☐ Pour in the wine, if using, and boil to reduce by a third. Cover with the cold water, bring back to the boil, skim and add the herbs, tied in a muslin cloth.

☐ Simmer for I hour, skimming from time to time. Strain through a fine sieve and leave to cool.

☐ Cool and store in a covered container in the fridge for 3 to 4 days or up to 2 months in the freezer.

VARIATIONS

CHICKEN DEMI-GLACE

By reducing the stock by half, to 2 ¼ cups/500 ml/18 fl oz you will obtain an even more flavourful stock (broth).

CHICKEN ESSENCE OR GLAZE

By reducing the stock further to I cup/200 ml/7 fl oz you will obtain an essence of chicken. This must be used very sparingly since it is extremely concentrated; it will greatly improve a sauce which lacks character.

**MAKES APPROX 2 ¼ CUPS/
500 ML/18 FL OZ**

*300 g/10 oz chicken giblets
I onion, peeled and quartered
I carrot, cut into chunks
I stick celery, chopped
6 black peppercorns
I bouquet garni
3 ¾ cups/900 ml/I ½ pt cold water*

QUICK CHICKEN GIBLET STOCK (BROTH)

While the chicken is roasting in the oven, this is an ideal quick stock to prepare for the gravy, or indeed, as a good stand-by light brown chicken stock for use in recipes.

A lot of oven-ready chickens are sold without the giblets, so it may be best to buy your chicken from the local butcher or poulterer and ask for the giblets to be included.

☐ Rinse the giblets under cold running water. Place in a saucepan with the remaining ingredients.

☐ Pour on the water, cover and steadily bring to the boil. Remove any scum at intervals with a spoon.

☐ Reduce the heat to a simmer and cook for a further 45 minutes. Continue to skim the surface.

☐ Strain the stock through a fine mesh sieve. Remove any visible fat.

GRAVY FOR ROAST CHICKEN

Because poultry has very little fat running through its meat, and can sometimes become a little dry, it is essential that a traditional roast chicken is accompanied with a tasty, moistening gravy.

There seems to be some resistance to making an old-fashioned gravy, which is a shame because it is almost as simple to prepare as a commercially produced gravy mix and tastes a lot more interesting.

Here are two recipes for gravy, both suitable for the succulent bird.

THIN GRAVY

- Transfer the roast chicken to a warm carving plate.
- Tilt the roasting pan and spoon the fat out. With a wooden spoon, scrape any sediment and crusty bits from the base of the pan. You should now be left with the chicken juices.
- Add a little wine, good stock (broth) or water and boil briskly for a minute to form a thin sauce.
- Season well with salt and freshly ground black pepper and serve immediately.

THICK GRAVY

- Transfer the roast chicken to a warm carving plate.
- Tilt the roasting pan and spoon the fat out, leaving only 1 or 2 tablespoonfuls of fat in with the chicken juices.
- Place the roasting pan over a high heat, and as soon as the juices sizzle, sprinkle on 15 ml/1 level tbsp plain (all purpose) flour. (This quantity will thicken 1¼ cups/300 ml/½ pint liquid.) Work the flour into the juices with a wooden spoon, scraping any sediment from the base at the same time.
- Gradually blend the stock into the floury paste and stir continuously until the gravy is smooth and has thickened. Season to taste, and serve immediately.

HOT WATER CRUST PASTRY

- Sift the flour into a warm mixing bowl with the salt and pepper. Make a well in the centre. Keep in a warm place.
- In a saucepan, heat together the lard, butter and water. When the liquid is just boiling and the fat has melted, pour into the flour and immediately mix vigorously with a wooden spoon, until smooth.
- Turn the pastry out onto a lightly floured board and knead until smooth. Wrap in cling film and leave to relax in a warm place for 20 minutes. Use at once.

4 cups/500 g/1 lb plain (all purpose) flour
½ cup/125 g/4 oz lard
½ cup/125 g/4 oz butter
⅔ cup/150 ml/¼ pt water (or milk)
pinch salt and freshly ground black pepper

15 ml/1 tbsp vegetable oil
1 onion, finely chopped
2 small Cox's Orange Pippin apples
(or sweet dessert apples)
10 ml/2 teaspoons fresh rosemary, chopped
2 cups/125 g/4 oz fresh white breadcrumbs
salt and freshly ground black pepper
1 egg yolk, beaten

STUFFINGS

Stuffings or forcemeats date back to the Middle Ages and their main purpose is to help keep the poultry flesh moist, to counteract any greasiness, and the herbs which are often included, were thought to aid digestion and stimulate the appetite.

Here are 4 different stuffings which are all suitable for poultry and provide a good basis for you to experiment and slightly amend the ingredients and flavourings. Each recipe yields sufficient for a 1.75 kg/4 lb chicken.

TO STUFF THE BREAST

☐ Starting at the neck end gently loosen the skin away from the breast to form a pocket.

☐ Using your fingers, work in some stuffing, evenly smoothing it down to form a rounded mound. Do not put too much stuffing in, as, during cooking, it will swell slightly and may break the skin.

☐ Fold the loose neck flap of skin back under the bird and secure with a cocktail stick or small skewer.

Simply spoon any remaining mixture into the bird's cavity or roll the stuffing into small balls and place in the roasting tin alongside the bird 30 minutes before the end of cooking.

NOTE

Remember to adjust the roasting times for stuffed birds (see page 7).

ROSEMARY & APPLE STUFFING

Heat the oil in a pan and sauté the onion until softened. Meanwhile, peel, core and finely chop the apples. Remove pan from heat and combine all the ingredients together.

1 cup/175 g/6 oz coarse oatmeal
¼ cup/50 g/2 oz butter, melted
1 large onion, finely chopped
2 pinches grated nutmeg
15 ml/1 tbsp mixed dried herbs
45 ml/3 tbsp whisky or stock (broth)
salt and freshly ground black pepper

OATMEAL STUFFING (SKIRLIE)

Combine all the ingredients together, adding a little extra liquid if necessary to make a moist mixture.

2 cups/125 g/4 oz fresh white breadcrumbs
½ stick celery, finely chopped
grated rind 1 small lemon
45 ml/3 tbsp freshly chopped parsley
10 ml/2 tsp freshly chopped thyme
salt and ground black pepper, to taste
2 tbsp/25 g/1 oz butter, melted
1 egg yolk, beaten

LEMON, PARSLEY & THYME STUFFING

Combine all the ingredients together in a bowl. Mix thoroughly.

2 tbsp/25 g/1 oz butter
1 medium onion, finely chopped
½ cup/125 g/4 oz dried apricots (non-soak variety)
¼ cup/50 g/2 oz blanched almonds, coarsely chopped
30 ml/2 tbsp chopped fresh chives, sage and parsley
1 cup/125 g/4 oz brown rice, cooked
1 egg yolk, beaten
salt and freshly ground black pepper, to taste

FRUIT & NUTTY RICE SALAD

Melt the butter in a pan and cook the onion until softened. Stir in the remaining ingredients, mixing thoroughly.

BREAD SAUCE

Bread sauce dates back to Medieval times and has remained a traditional accompaniment to roast chicken and turkey ever since. The purpose of the breadcrumbs was originally to thicken a sauce in the absence of a stove for simmering and reducing.

☐ Gently warm the milk in a saucepan, to just under boiling point. Remove.

☐ Stick the cloves into the onion, and add to the milk together with the peppercorns, bayleaf and mace. Leave the milk to stand for 30 minutes to allow the flavours to infuse.

☐ Add the breadcrumbs, butter and seasoning and return to a very gentle heat for 10 minutes. Remove the onion, cloves, peppercorns, bayleaf and mace. Check seasoning. Stir in the cream (optional).

☐ Serve immediately in a sauce boat to accompany the roast chicken.

NOTE
Bread sauce is not suitable for freezing.

MARINADES FOR BARBECUED CHICKEN

A marinade is, very often, a highly seasoned or flavoured liquid – perhaps with the addition of spices, herbs or citrus fruits. Marinating flavours food such as fish, meat, game and poultry and even vegetables. It can tenderize tougher cuts, give moisture to dry meats and preserves the food for a day or two longer than normal. The marinade can also act as a barbecue sauce, to baste the grilled or roast meats.

The first two liquid marinades are excellent for chicken. Simply mix the ingredients together. Quantities are enough for a 1.75 kg/3½ lb chicken or equivalent parts.

☐ Lay the chicken joints or pieces in a shallow dish. Pour over the marinade.

☐ Turn the chicken, to coat thoroughly.

☐ Cover with cling film (plastic wrap) and leave at room temperature for 2 to 3 hours, or chill for 8 hours, preferably overnight.

☐ Drain the chicken and cook accordingly. Baste the chicken with the remaining marinade, turning the chicken frequently.

If you are wanting to roast or grill a whole or jointed chicken with a difference, the simple and speedy infusion of flavours given by a dry marinade is perfect. Because of the high salt content, the marinade should only be on the chicken for 1 hour.

☐ Crush the garlic cloves with the flat blade of a heavy chopping knife, or alternatively, use a pestle and mortar.

☐ Add the other ingredients and work them together until they are reduced to a paste.

☐ Spread the surface of the chicken with the marinade. Cover and leave to stand for 1 hour.

☐ Scrape off and discard the marinade before cooking the chicken.

TO MAKE 1¼ CUP/300 ML/ ½ PINT

1¼ cups/300 ml/½ pt milk
1 medium onion, peeled
4 cloves
6 black peppercorns
1 bayleaf
1 small piece mace
1 cup/50 g/2 oz fresh white breadcrumbs
2 tbsp/25 g/1 oz butter
salt and white pepper
15 ml/1 tbsp single (light) cream (optional)

WHITE WINE MARINADE

¼ cup/60 ml/4 tbsp white wine
30 ml/2 tbsp olive oil
30 ml/2 tbsp lemon juice
5 ml/1 tsp mustard powder
1 clove garlic, finely chopped
4 black peppercorns
1 bayleaf
1 sprig tarragon (optional)
1 strip lemon peel

YOGURT MARINADE

⅔ cup/150 ml/¼ pt natural yogurt
30 ml/2 tbsp tomato ketchup
30 ml/2 tbsp olive oil
15 ml/1 tbsp Worcestershire sauce
10 ml/2 tsp clear honey
5 ml/1 tsp mustard powder
dash Tabasco
1 shallot, finely chopped
2 cloves garlic, finely chopped

DRY CHICKEN MARINADE

4 cloves garlic
5 ml/1 tsp dried thyme
2.5 ml/½ tsp ground bayleaves
8 black peppercorns, crushed
30 ml/2 tbsp coarse salt
15 ml/1 tbsp lemon juice

SOUPS, STARTERS, PÂTÉS & TERRINES

SERVES 4

30 ml/2 tbsp vegetable oil
1 onion, halved and sliced
1 clove garlic, finely chopped
1 carrot, peeled and diced
1 potato, peeled and diced
50 g/2 oz green (string or snap) beans, trimmed and chopped
2 chicken thighs, skinned
1 sharp eating apple, peeled, cored and diced
10 ml/2 tsp hot curry paste
10 ml/2 tsp tomato purée (paste)
2.5 ml/½ tsp ground ginger
2.5 ml/½ tsp ground nutmeg
4 cloves
45 ml/3 tbsp lemon juice
15 ml/1 tbsp Worcestershire sauce
5 cups/1.2 l/2 pt chicken stock (broth)
salt and freshly ground black pepper

MULLIGATAWNY

A native of Tamil Nadu, Southern India, the name 'Milaku' (pepper) and 'tanni' (water) is a fitting description of this highly spiced substantial soup. This was one of the many recipes the British Raj brought back to Britain and adapted for 'home cooking'. Serve accompanied with plain boiled rice.

☐ Heat the oil in a large, heavy-based saucepan. Add the onion and garlic and cook for 2 to 3 minutes, or until the onions start to soften.

☐ Add the carrot, potato, beans and chicken thighs and cook, stirring, for a further 4 to 5 minutes or until the chicken is lightly coloured.

☐ Stir in the diced apple, curry paste, tomato purée (paste), ginger, nutmeg and cloves. Cover and 'sweat' over a moderate heat for 3 to 4 minutes. Scrape loose any sediment from the base of the pan.

☐ Add the lemon juice, Worcestershire sauce and stock (broth). Bring to the boil, then cover and simmer for 20 to 30 minutes or until the chicken is tender. Season to taste.

☐ Lift out the chicken thighs with a slotted spoon. Take the flesh off the bone, break up into small strips and return to the soup.

☐ Serve hot. If preferred, the soup can be puréed and served hot or chilled, garnished with a swirl of natural yogurt.

COCK-A-LEEKIE SOUP

Scotland is thought to be the home of this substantial soup – although the Welsh may agree to differ! The bird that ended up in the stock pot may originally have been the loser of a cock-fight. Long simmering is required but the result is well worth waiting for.

□ Place the chicken in a large, heavy-based saucepan. Add the onion, carrots, celery, bayleaf, bouquet garni, peppercorns and salt. Cover with the water.

□ Bring the pan very gently to the boil, skim, and then simmer for about 2 hours or until the chicken is tender. Strain off the stock, discarding the cooked vegetables, and leave to cool, then chill in the refrigerator until the fat hardens and can be easily removed. Alternatively, clean off all the grease from the hot stock with absorbent kitchen paper (paper towel). Remove the skin from the chicken and cut the flesh into thin strips.

□ Melt the butter in a large pan, add the leeks and spring onions (scallions) and cook over a low heat for 10 minutes. Add the rice and allspice and cook for a further 5 minutes. Pour on the skimmed stock, bring to the boil and simmer for 15 minutes. Add the chicken and simmer for a further 10 minutes, season to taste, mix in the parsley and serve.

SERVES 4 TO 6

1 small boiling or roasting chicken (approx. 1.1–1.5 kg/2½–3½ lb)
1 onion, quartered
2 carrots, chopped
1 stick celery, chopped
1 bayleaf
1 bouquet garni
6 peppercorns
5 ml/1 tsp salt
7½ cups/1.75 l/3 pt water
2 tbsp/25 g/1 oz butter
4 leeks, trimmed and thinly sliced
2 spring onions (scallions), trimmed and thinly sliced
¼ cup/25 g/1 oz long grain rice
pinch allspice
15 ml/1 tbsp chopped parsley

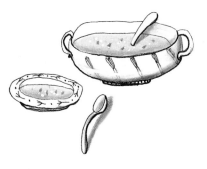

ORIENTAL CHICKEN NOODLE SOUP

Soup is included in almost every meal in Thailand and China and, contrary to Western custom, the soup is eaten together with other dishes, or even at the end of the meal. What is common worldwide, though, is that the basis of a good soup is the stock.

□ Cut the chicken into thin strips. Soak the mushrooms in warm water for 15 minutes. Drain well, squeezing out excess moisture. Cut away and discard the stems and shred the caps.

□ Bring the chicken stock to a steady simmer. Add the chicken, mushrooms, noodles, sugar, soy sauce, sherry or rice wine and pepper to taste. Simmer for 15 minutes or until the chicken and noodles are tender.

□ Stir in the spring onions, red chilli (chili) flakes, chopped coriander (cilantro) and sesame oil

□ Pour into individual bowls and serve immediately.

SERVES 4 TO 6

250 g/8 oz boneless chicken meat (breast or thigh)
4 dried Chinese mushrooms
4½ cups/1.2 l/2 pt chicken stock (broth) (see page 12)
2 bundles rice vermicelli noodles (approx. 150 g/5 oz)
10 ml/2 tsp sugar
30 ml/2 tsp dark soy sauce
45 ml/3 tbsp dry sherry or rice wine
white pepper
4 spring onions (scallions), cut diagonally into 2 cm/1 in strips
15 ml/1 tbsp dried red chilli (chili) flakes
15 ml/1 tbsp fresh coriander (cilantro), chopped
10 ml/2 tsp sesame oil

SERVES 6 TO 8

250 g/8 oz chicken livers
15 ml/1 tbsp vegetable oil
375 g/12 oz chicken breast, skinned
30 ml/2 tbsp medium sherry
15 ml/1 tbsp brandy
a few black peppercorns, roughly crushed
500 g/1 lb minced pork
1 egg
1 clove garlic, crushed (minced)
5 ml/1 tsp salt
¼ cup/60 ml/4 tbsp walnuts coarsely chopped

GARNISH
assorted salad leaves
spring onion (scallion) flowers (optional)

Oven temperature: 190 °C/375 °F/Gas 5

CHICKEN AND WALNUT TERRINE

The French word 'terrine' originally meant an earthenware dish, but nowadays refers to its contents. This needs to be made a day or two in advance to develop the flavours, and should be served cold, sliced, with a salad garnish and wholemeal bread.

☐ Sauté half the chicken liver in the oil until just browned. Remove and cut into thin strips. Cut the chicken breast into thin strips and put in a bowl with the cooked livers, the sherry, brandy and peppercorns. Cover and leave to marinade for 2 hours.

☐ Put the remaining chicken livers and the pork in a food processor and blend together with the egg, garlic and salt, until the mixture is smooth.

☐ Place one third of this mixture in a lightly greased 5 cup/1.2 1/2 pt terrine or loaf tin (pan), and cover with half the chicken strips and half the walnuts.

☐ Cover with another third of the pork mixture, and then the rest of the chicken strips and walnuts. Spread the remaining pork mixture over the top. Cover with foil.

☐ Place on a baking tray (cookie sheet), and bake for 1 hour. Cool, top off any liquid and then chill, preferably overnight.

☐ Serve in slices, garnished with an assortment of salad leaves and, if you like, spring onion (scallion) flowers.

CHICKEN LIVERS IN JACKETS

Inexpensive to make and quick to produce, these little rolls of crisp bacon encasing chicken livers will soon vanish with the cocktails! The fruits listed below are just a suggestion of what to serve with the chicken livers, but almost any fruit works well.

Chicken Livers in Jackets

MAKES APPROX 36

300 g–375 g/10 oz–12 oz chicken livers
16 rashers streaky bacon, derinded

TO SERVE
1 kiwi fruit
1 banana
drived apricot halves (non-soak variety)
bamboo skewers/cocktail sticks

Oven temperature: 220 °C/425 °F/Gas 7

☐ Drain the chicken livers, if necessary, and remove any threads. Cut each into pieces the size of a small walnut.

☐ Using the back of a heavy knife, stretch the bacon rashers lengthways on a large chopping board. Cut each rasher into 2 to 3 equal lengths, each long enough to wrap around a piece of chicken liver.

☐ Roll the bacon lengths around the chicken livers. Push a thin bamboo skewer (pre-soaked for ½ hour to prevent burning) through the centre of each roll. Lay on a rack in a grill pan or small roasting tin. Cook for 10 to 15 minutes in the oven, or under a preheated grill (broiler), until sizzling and crisp. Remove skewers.

☐ Meanwhile, prepare the fruit. Cut the banana into thick slices, halve the kiwi fruit lengthwise and cut into thick slices.

☐ Thread each bacon roll and a piece of fruit onto cocktail sticks and serve immediately.

CHICKEN, PRAWN (SHRIMP) & SWEETCORN CHOWDER

A meal on its own. The word 'chowder' derives from the French Canadian cooking utensil 'Chaudière'. Originally Newfoundland fishermen made a stew of cod and potatoes, but the recipe developed to include clams, scallops and salmon. In this version, I hope I am forgiven for introducing chicken to the 'chaudière'. The combination marries well and makes the expensive shellfish ingredients go further.

☐ Heat the oil in a large saucepan and cook the onions for 10 minutes, or until softened, but not browned. Add the diced potato and nutmeg and cook for a further 5 minutes. Stir in the stock, cover and simmer for 15 minutes. Purée in a liquidizer. Season to taste.

☐ Fry the bacon in its own fat until well browned. Add the chicken and cook for a further 2 minutes. Stir in the sweetcorn kernels, and prawns (shrimp) or scallops. Add the puréed stock mixture and blend in the milk. Simmer gently for 10 minutes or until the chicken is tender. Season to taste.

☐ Serve in deep bowls, garnished with a swirl of cream (or fromage frais) and a dusting of chopped chervil. Accompany with crusty brown bread.

CHICKEN AND SPRING ONION (SCALLION) CANÂPÉS

These canâpés are straightforward, disappear as quickly as they are made, and are low in calories too!

☐ Halve the chicken breasts, put each between 2 sheets of dampened greaseproof paper and flatten to a thickness of 1.25 cm/½ in. Halve each piece lengthwise, to give a total of 8 pieces.

☐ Place a spring onion (scallion) lengthways on each chicken piece, and roll up tightly. Secure with cotton or string.

☐ Mix together the marinade ingredients in a shallow dish and add the chicken rolls. Cover and chill for 2 to 3 hours, turning the rolls occasionally.

☐ Steam the chicken rolls for 5 minutes, or cook in a 650W microwave oven for 4 to 5 minutes on HIGH. (Position the rolls around the outer edge of a large plate.)

☐ Return the cooked chicken to the marinade to cool for 1 hour, turning frequently to coat them.

☐ Remove the string and cut the rolls at a diagonal into 1.25 cm/½ in slices. Dust with paprika and arrange on a serving platter. Garnish with some chilli (chili) flowers if you like and sprigs of fresh coriander (cilantro) or dill.

SERVES 4 TO 6

30 ml/2 tbsp vegetable oil
2 medium onions, finely chopped
2 medium potatoes, peeled and diced
2 pinches grated nutmeg
750 ml/1 ¼ pt chicken stock (broth)
salt and freshly ground black pepper
50 g/2 oz streaky smoked bacon, derinded and chopped
1 boneless chicken breast (approx. 150 g/5 oz) skinned and sliced in strips
1 small can (approx. 225 g/7 oz) sweetcorn kernels, drained
125 g/4 oz peeled prawns (shrimp) (or 4 scallops, chopped)
1 ¼ cups/300 ml/½ pt milk
¼ cup/60 ml/4 tbsp single (light) cream or fromage frais
freshly chopped chervil to garnish

Chicken, Prawn (Shrimp) and Sweetcorn Chowder

MAKES 35 TO 40

2 boneless chicken breasts, skinned (approx. 175 g/6 oz each)
1 bunch spring onions (scallions), trimmed
MARINADE
¼ cup/60 ml/4 tbsp light soy sauce
30 ml/2 tbsp sherry vinegar
GARNISH
Chilli (chili) flowers (optional)
fresh coriander (cilantro) or dill

175 g/6 oz cooked chicken breast
1 ½ cups/350 g/12 oz low fat cream cheese or
fromage frais
2 eggs (size 1) plus 1 egg yolk
salt and white pepper
175 g/6 oz carrots, cooked and chopped
2.5 ml/½ tsp ground coriander
SAUCE
2 large sweet red or yellow (bell) peppers
1 small shallot or ½ a small sweet onion,
finely chopped
1 clove garlic, finely chopped
2 cups/500 ml/16 fl oz vegetable or chicken stock
(broth)
pinch sugar
salt and pepper, to taste
GARNISH
fresh chervil
baby carrots with leaves, when available

CHICKEN AND CARROT TIMBALES WITH SWEET (BELL) PEPPER SAUCE

A bright and colourful start to a meal, best served just warm. The sauce can be made well in advance and chilled until required, but the delicate creamy timbales are ideally eaten freshly made.

If you have the time, divide the sauce ingredients and make one half with red and the other half with yellow peppers.

☐ Put the chicken, half the cheese and one egg in a good processor or liquidizer and process until smooth. Season to taste. Transfer to a small bowl.

☐ Repeat the process with the carrots, the remaining cheese and egg and the egg yolk. Season to taste and stir in the ground coriander.

☐ Lightly grease 6 small timbale (thimble-shaped) moulds and divide half the chicken mixture between the bases of each mould. Then spoon on the carrot purée and finally the remaining chicken mixture. Tap the side of each mould gently to level out the surface.

☐ Place the moulds in a roasting tin half filled with water, cover with foil and cook for 40 minutes or until lightly set. (A wooden cocktail stick will come out of the mousse clean when it is cooked.) Leave to stand for 5 minutes before unmoulding.

☐ Meanwhile, make the sauce. Cut the peppers into pieces. Sweat the onions and garlic in a covered pan with a couple of tablespoons of stock. (Do not brown the onions.)

☐ Add the peppers and stock and simmer, uncovered, for 15 to 20 minutes or until the peppers are tender. Liquidize to a smooth purée and season to taste with salt, pepper and sugar. Leave to cool slightly.

☐ Spoon the warm sauce over a plate. (If you are using two colours, spoon one sauce on one side of the plate and the second colour on the other side. Gently tip the plate just enough to run the sauces into one another.)

☐ Carefully unmould the timbales and place in the centre of each plate. Garnish with sprigs of fresh chervil and a small baby carrot, and serve immediately.

CHICKEN QUENELLES WITH SORREL SAUCE

Quenelles are small, egg-shapes of a mousse-like, finely minced meat mixture, poached in a simmering liquid. The quenelle mixture can be prepared in advance, but must be cooked at the very last moment. Vary the sauce according to the availability of fresh herbs. Tarragon, mixed herbs, even watercress, are equally good.

- ☐ Cut up the chicken and put it into a food processor and work until finely chopped.
- ☐ Season, add the egg and egg white and process again until smooth. Fold in the fromage frais and chives. Adjust the seasoning, turn onto a wetted plate and chill for 3 to 4 hours.
- ☐ Meanwhile, make the sauce. Remove the larger stalks from the sorrel and blanch the leaves in ½ cup/125 ml/4 fl oz of boiling stock (broth). Allow to cool, then purée in a liquidizer together with the fromage frais. Season to taste.
- ☐ Boil the remaining stock until reduced by half. Stir into the sorrel sauce, and keep warm.
- ☐ To make the quenelles, mould the chilled chicken into oval shapes by using 2 wet dessertspoons. Bring the 4½ cups/1.2 l/2 pt of stock (broth) to a simmer in a large frying pan (skillet). Gently slide each 'quenelle' into the simmering stock and poach for about 2 minutes on each side. Drain on absorbent paper (paper towel).
- ☐ Spoon the warmed sauce onto 4 individual plates, top with the quenelles and garnish with fresh chives. Serve immediately.

SERVES 4

375 g/12 oz chicken breast, skinned
1 egg plus 1 egg white
½ cup/125 ml/4 fl oz fromage frais or double (heavy) cream
salt and freshly ground pepper
15 ml/1 tbsp fresh chives, chopped
4½ cups/1.2 l/2 pt chicken stock (broth)

SAUCE
3 cups/250 g/8 oz sorrel leave
1 ½ cups/375 ml/12 fl oz chicken stock (broth)
¼ cup/60 ml/4 tbsp fromage frais
salt and freshly ground black pepper

GARNISH
fresh chives

SERVES 4

500 g/1 lb chicken livers
1/3 cup/90 ml/6 tbsp ruby port
2 cloves garlic, crushed (minced)
10 ml/2 tsp fresh thyme, chopped
2.5 ml/1/2 tsp grated nutmeg
2 tbsp/25 g/1 oz butter
1/4 cup/60 ml/4 tbsp fromage frais or double (heavy)
cream
salt and freshly ground black pepper
5 ml/1 tsp powdered gelatine (gelatin)
2/3 cup/150 ml/1/4 pt chicken stock (broth)

GARNISH
bay leaves
peppercorns
stuffed olives

Oven temperature: 180 °C/350 °F/Gas 4

CHICKEN LIVER PÂTÉ

A very good pâté – quick to make and best served with melba toast or french bread. Try it too, as a cânapé, spooned into small mushroom caps or hollowed out cherry tomatoes.

☐ Trim and wash the livers, and cut in half. Put them in a bowl with the port, garlic, thyme and nutmeg. Mix the ingredients well, cover and marinade for 2 hours. Drain the livers, reserving the juices.

☐ Melt the butter in a frying pan, add the drained livers, and sauté for a few minutes or until the livers change colour.

☐ Add the reserved juices and simmer, uncovered, for a further minute. Cool slightly. Season to taste.

☐ Blend or process the liver mixture together with the fromage frais or cream until smooth. Pour into a small serving dish (or 4 individual ramekin dishes). Cover and place in a roasting tin half filled with water. Cook for 40 minutes.

☐ Sprinkle the gelatine (gelatin) into the hot chicken stock. Dissolve over a pan of hot water (or microwave on HIGH at 600W for 30 seconds). Cool to room temperature, or until just syrupy.

☐ Arrange the bayleaves, peppercorns and stuffed olive slices on top of the pâté. Carefully spoon a thin layer of the gelatine (gelatin) mixture over. Chill until set.

NOTE

The made up pâté will freeze for up to 2 months, after cooking, but before the gelatine (gelatin) is applied.

CHICKEN AND SPINACH TERRINE

A perfect start to a dinner party, or as a main course for a summer lunch. Serve on its own, or with new potatoes and a fresh crisp green salad.

- ☐ For the spinach mixture, mix the spinach with nutmeg, salt and pepper to taste. Blend in the fromage frais and egg yolks.
- ☐ Dissolve the gelatine (gelatin) in 30 ml/2 tbsp water (place in a basin over a pan of simmering water). Allow to cool slightly before stirring into the spinach mixture.
- ☐ For the chicken mixture, heat the oil and stir-fry the minced chicken for 4 to 5 minutes. Do not allow it to brown.
- ☐ Add the garlic, green peppercorns, salt and pepper to taste, and the Vermouth. Bubble briskly for 1 minute.
- ☐ Blend the chicken in a liquidizer or food processor until smooth. Stir the pistachio nuts and fromage frais into the chicken mixture.
- ☐ Dissolve the gelatine (gelatin) in 45 ml/3 tbsp water (as above) and add to the chicken mixture; blend well.
- ☐ Put half the chicken mixture into a lightly oiled and lined 1 kg/2 lb loaf tin (pan), cover carefully with the spinach mixture, and spread the remaining chicken mixture over the top. Chill until the terrine is firm enough to slice.
- ☐ Meanwhile, make the sauce. Put the yogurt, watercress and garlic into a liquidizer or food processor and blend until smooth. Stir in the white wine and season to taste.
- ☐ Carefully unmould (unmold) the set terrine and cut into slices. Place a slice on each serving plate, and spoon a pool of sauce around the terrine. Garnish with a few extra green peppercorns or a sprig of fresh dill.

SERVES 8 TO 10

SPINACH MIXTURE

500 g/1 lb cooked spinach, well drained and chopped
freshly grated nutmeg
salt and freshly ground black pepper
⅔ cup/150 ml/¼ pt fromage frais (low fat)
2 egg yolks
10 ml/2 tsp powdered gelatine (gelatin)

CHICKEN MIXTURE

15 ml/1 tbsp vegetable oil
700 g/1½ lb boneless chicken, minced
1 clove garlic, crushed (minced)
5 ml/1 tsp green peppercorns
salt and freshly ground black pepper
¼ cup/60 ml/4 tbsp dry Vermouth
25 g/1 oz pistachio nuts
¾ cup/175 ml/6 fl oz fromage frais (low fat)
15 ml/3 tsp powdered gelatine (gelatin)

SAUCE

scant cup/200 ml/⅓ pt thick natural yogurt
(preferably low fat)
1 bunch watercress, washed and trimmed
1 whole clove garlic, peeled
¼ cup/60 ml/4 tbsp dry white wine
salt and freshly ground black pepper

GARNISH

a few green peppercorns or a sprig of dill

SALADS & COLD CHICKEN DISHES

SERVES 4

4 chicken breasts (approx. 150 g/5 oz each), skinned and boned
1 ¼ cups/300 ml/½ pt chicken stock (broth) or dry white wine

MARINADE

30 ml/2 tbsp teriyaki marinade (or soy sauce)
15 ml/1 tbsp dry sherry
15 ml/1 tbsp clear honey
5 ml/1 tsp grated fresh ginger
1 clove garlic, crushed (minced)

½ sweet red (bell) pepper, deseeded and cut into strips
1 small carrot, cut into thin strips
4 spring onions (scallions), trimmed and halved lengthways
1 stick celery, chopped
4 water chestnuts (canned), sliced
4 baby sweetcorn, blanched and halved lengthways
15 ml/1 tbsp sesame seeds, toasted

DRESSING

30 ml/2 tbsp sherry vinegar
30 ml/2 tbsp vegetable oil
15 ml/1 tbsp teriyaki marinade (or soy sauce)
15 ml/1 tbsp dry sherry
15 ml/1 tbsp stem ginger syrup
2.5 ml/½ tsp sesame oil

ORIENTAL CHICKEN SALAD

This salad can be prepared up to 12 hours in advance and is an ideal lunch dish or one to include in a buffet table – in which case this quantity would serve 8 to 10.

□ Place the chicken in a shallow dish. Put the marinade ingredients in a screw top jar. Shake vigorously, then pour onto the chicken. Cover and chill for several hours.

□ Remove the chicken with a slotted spoon; discard the marinade. Put the stock (broth) in a small pan, add the chicken, cover and simmer for 10 minutes. Drain and cool the chicken, then cut into thin strips.

□ Combine the chicken with the vegetable and salad ingredients. Sprinkle over the sesame seeds.

□ Shake the dressing ingredients together in a screw top jar and pour over the chicken salad. Serve.

SMOKED CHICKEN, BACON AND PRAWN (SHRIMP) SALAD

This salad makes the perfect starter, as it can be prepared well in advance and assembled at the last minute. Alternatively, serve this as a light lunch for two.

☐ First make the dressing; combine the first five ingredients in a screw top jar and shake vigorously until well blended. Season with salt and pepper to taste.

☐ Slice the chicken breast into thin strips. Place in a bowl together with the prawns (shrimp) and mushrooms and pour over the dressing. Carefully fold the ingredients together. Cover and chill.

☐ Grill the bacon until crisp. Crumble into a bowl.

☐ Line four individual serving plates with an assortment of lettuce leaves. Drain the chicken mixture and spoon on top of the salad. Sprinkle with bacon, and garnish with fresh snipped chives.

SERVES 4 TO 5

DRESSING
⅓ cup/90 ml/6 tbsp sunflower oil
30 ml/2 tbsp white wine vinegar
pinch dry mustard
1 shallot or ½ a small, sweet onion, finely chopped
¼ cup/60 ml/4 tbsp chopped fresh parsley
salt and freshly ground black pepper

175 g/6 oz smoked chicken breast, cooked
175 g/6 oz peeled prawns (shrimp)
½ cup/50 g/2 oz button mushrooms, sliced thinly
3 rashers lean bacon, derinded

GARNISH
Selection of lettuce leaves
fresh chives

Minted Chicken with Melon Medley

Smoked Chicken, Bacon and Prawn (Shrimp) Salad

MINTED CHICKEN AND MELON MEDLEY

Nowadays, we are fortunate to have a variety of melons available throughout the year. This fruit contrasts well with chicken, both in flavour and moistness. Serve this salad accompanied with crusty garlic bread for a light lunch.

☐ Put the chicken, grape juice and salt and pepper to taste in a pan. Bring to the boil, then simmer for 10 minutes, or until the chicken is tender. (Turn the chicken once during cooking.) Drain and cool.

☐ Using a Parisienne cutter, scoop out the flesh of the melons to form neat balls. Alternatively, cut the flesh into 2.5 cm/1 in cubes. Place in a bowl with the halved grapes. Dice the chicken and add to the fruit, together with the cheese.

☐ Shake the dressing ingredients together in a screw-top jar and gently fold into the salad. Chill for 30 minutes before serving, garnished with sprigs of fresh mint.

SERVES 4 TO 6

6 chicken breasts, boneless and skinned
(each approximately 150 g/5 oz)
1¼ cups/300 ml/1½ pt white grape juice
salt and freshly ground black pepper
½ ripe rock melon (Charentais or Honeydew),
deseeded
½ ripe Ogen melon, deseeded
175 g/6 oz seedless red grapes
125 g/4 oz feta cheese, cubed

DRESSING
30 ml/2 tbsp light olive oil
15 ml/1 tbsp grape juice
15 ml/1 tbsp lemon juice
15 ml/1 tbsp fromage frais or single (light) cream
15 ml/1 tbsp each freshly chopped mint and chives
salt and freshly ground black pepper

GARNISH
fresh mint sprigs

SERVES 4

500 g/1 lb cooked chicken meat, in small chunks
2 ripe avocados
15 ml/1 tbsp lemon juice
4 tomatoes, skinned
2 spring onions (scallions), chopped
30 ml/2 tbsp chopped parsley
50 g/2 oz cashew nuts, toasted

GARLIC VINAIGRETTE

45 ml/3 tbsp groundnut oil
15 ml/1 tbsp white wine vinegar
5 ml/1 tsp Dijon mustard
1 clove garlic, crushed (minced)
2.5 ml/½ tsp caster (fine) sugar
salt and freshly ground black pepper

AVOCADO AND CHICKEN SALAD

This is a quick, yet delicious, way of using up any left-over cooked chicken – a perfect summer lunch. Try ringing the changes with mango instead of avocado.

☐ Split the avocado in half, remove the stone (pit) and skin and cut into neat slices. Brush with the lemon juice to prevent discoloration.

☐ Slice each tomato and arrange alternately with the avocado around the outer edge of a flat serving plate, as shown.

☐ Mix the chicken with the spring onions, parsley and nuts. Whisk together the Garlic Vinaigrette ingredients. There should be enough to coat the chicken well.

☐ Pile the mixture in the centre of the plate. Brush any remaining dressing over the avocado and tomato slices. Garnish with a sprinkling of parsley.

Avocado and Chicken Salad

Hot Chicken and Spinach Salad

SERVES 4

175 g/6 oz fresh young spinach leaves
6 small spring onions (scallions), trimmed and sliced
30 ml/2 tbsp toasted hazelnuts, chopped
2 small courgettes (zucchini), thinly sliced
2 boneless chicken breasts, skinned
(approx. 150 g/5 oz each)
⅓ cup/90 ml/6 tbsp light olive oil
1 small onion, finely chopped
1 clove garlic, finely chopped
30 ml/2 tbsp white wine vinegar
salt and freshly ground black pepper
15 ml/1 tbsp fresh tarragon, chopped
(or 5 ml/1 tsp dried)
1 small sweet red (bell) pepper, deseeded and diced

HOT CHICKEN AND SPINACH SALAD

☐ Rinse and lightly shake the spinach leaves. Tear into pieces and place in a bowl or on individual serving plates. Sprinkle on the spring onions (scallions), hazelnuts and courgettes (zucchini).

☐ Cut the chicken into thin strips. Heat two thirds of the oil in a large, shallow pan and briskly stir-fry the chicken with the onion and garlic until just tender.

☐ Stir in the remaining olive oil, wine vinegar, salt and pepper and tarragon. Allow to cook for a further minutes. Spoon the hot chicken and dressing over the salad ingredients.

☐ Sprinkle with the diced sweet red (bell) pepper and serve immediately.

ORANGE, CHICORY (BELGIAN ENDIVE) AND CHICKEN SALAD

Buy either the red or green chicory (Belgian endive) for this recipe – the leaves can be used as 'scoops' to eat the salad. Serve on its own or with a simple tomato salad.

☐ Cook the rice according to instructions. Drain thoroughly and fork in the olive oil, fresh tarragon, orange juice and 2.5 ml/½ tsp of the orange rind. Leave to cool. Cover and chill.

☐ Beat the yogurt and cream cheese together with 2.5 ml/½ tsp orange rind. Fold in the chicken, toasted almonds, chives, coriander seeds, and season with salt and pepper to taste. Cover and chill.

☐ Arrange the chicory (Belgian endive) leaves around the outer edge of a shallow round serving dish. Spoon a circle of rice around the base of the chicory and pile the chicken mixture in the centre.

☐ Garnish with julienne strips of orange rind and sprigs of fresh tarragon.

SERVES 4

2 cups/250 g/8 oz brown rice
15 ml/1 tbsp olive oil
15 ml/1 tbsp chopped fresh tarragon (or parsley)
grated rind and juice of 1 large orange
⅔ cup/150 ml/½ pt low fat yogurt
¼ cup/50 g/2 oz low fat cream cheese
500 g/1 lb cooked chicken, cubed
25 g/1 oz flaked almonds, toasted
15 ml/1 tbsp fresh chives, snipped
10 ml/2 tsp coriander (cilantro) seeds, crushed
salt and freshly ground black pepper
2–3 heads chicory (Belgian endive)

GARNISH
julienne of orange rind (see Glossary p. 93)
fresh tarragon or parsley

NEGOMBO PINEAPPLE AND CHICKEN SALAD

Named after a village in 'Paradise' – Sri Lanka – abundant with fresh sweet pineapples, coconuts and spice plantations. Serve as a light lunch, or part of a buffet, accompanied with poppadums.

☐ Halve the pineapple (and leafy top) lengthways. Carefully scooop out the flesh, cut into neat cubes and place in a large bowl. Reserve the shells.

☐ Blend the mayonnaise, curry powder and cumin together and gently fold into the pineapple with the remaining ingredients. Season to taste. Cover and chill for 2 hours, to allow the flavours to develop.

☐ Divide the mixture between the two pineapple shells, and serve garnished with the strips of tomato and fresh coriander (cilantro) sprigs.

SERVES 2 TO 4

1 medium pineapple
45 ml/3 tbsp low calorie mayonnaise
15 ml/1 tbsp mild curry powder
2.5 ml/½ tsp ground cumin
250 g/8 oz cooked chicken, cubed
2 sticks celery, washed and diced
2 spring onions (scallions), trimmed and chopped
1 medium potato, boiled and cubed
1 sharp eating apple, peeled, cored and diced
15 ml/1 tbsp coconut flakes, toasted
6 cardamon pods, seeds only, lightly crushed
15 ml/1 tbsp fresh coriander (cilantro), chopped
⅔ cup/150 ml/¼ pt low fat natural yogurt
salt and freshly ground black pepper

GARNISH
1 tomato, skinned, deseeded and cut into strips
fresh coriander (cilantro) sprigs

SERVES 2 TO 4

2 boneless chicken breasts (approx. 175 g/6 oz each)

SAUCE

scant cup/200 ml/7 fl oz milk
small carrot, finely chopped
½ small onion, finely chopped
½ stick celery, finely chopped
1 bayleaf
1 ½ tbsp/20 g/¾ oz butter
scant ¼ cup/20 g/¾ oz plain (all purpose flour)
15 ml/1 tbsp double (heavy) cream
salt and white pepper
¼ cup/60 ml/4 tbsp powdered aspic
2.5 ml/½ tsp powdered gelatine (gelatin)

GARNISH

fresh herbs
2 cups/450 ml/¾ pt made up aspic

Oven temperature: 190 °C/375 °F/Gas 5

Chicken and Kiwi Fruit Salad with Strawberry Dressing

SERVES 4

2 chicken breasts (approx. 175 g/ 6 oz each), cooked
and skinned
2 kiwi fruit, peeled and thinly sliced
assorted salad leaves, washed

DRESSING

125 g/4 oz strawberries, hulled
5 ml/1 tsp grated orange rind
¼ cup/60 ml/4 tbsp light olive oil
30 ml/2 tbsp red wine vinegar
salt and freshly ground black pepper

GARNISH

8 whole strawberries
5 ml/1 tsp green peppercorns, coarsely crushed

CHICKEN CHAUDFROID

Chicken Chaudfroid looks very eyecatching on a buffet table, but does need a patient and attentive cook. However, the effort is well worth it! Whole roast chickens or, as in this recipe, chicken breasts or fillets (filets) can be used.

☐ Wrap the chicken breasts in foil and bake 'en papillote' in a roasting pan with a little water for 20 minutes until just cooked. (Or they can be steamed for 30 minutes.) Remove the skin, lay the breasts on a board, cover with cling film (plastic wrap) and flatten slightly under a weighted plate, and chill.

☐ For the sauce, bring milk to the boil, pour over the vegetables and bayleaf and leave to infuse for ½ hour. Strain.

☐ In a pan, melt the butter and blend in the flour. Stir well, cooking for 1 to 2 minutes, then gradually add the strained milk, stirring well between each addition. Stir in the cream, season and remove from the heat.

☐ Put the aspic powder in a small bowl with just enough water to cover and place in a saucepan of simmering water. Add the powdered gelatine (gelatin) and stir until dissolved. Add to the white sauce. Strain the sauce into a bowl and cool until slightly thickened.

☐ Place the chilled chicken breasts on a wire cake rack and spoon a layer of sauce over them. Refrigerate until the sauce has set.

☐ Repeat with successive coats of almost set sauce (if it becomes too thick it can be warmed gently) until a good surface has been formed.

☐ For the garnish make up the aspic according to the manufacturer's instructions and pour two thirds into a small baking tin (pan) to set. Leave the remainder until almost set.

☐ Decorate the chicken breasts with fresh herbs and coat with the almost-set aspic jelly.

☐ Serve the chicken surrounded by the set aspic, coarsely chopped.

VARIATION

Alternative decoration for the chicken can include flowers with 'petals' cut from hard boiled (hard cooked) egg white or green and red sweet (bell) peppers. Make yellow centres with hard boiled (hard cooked) egg yolk.

CHICKEN AND KIWI FRUIT SALAD WITH STRAWBERRY DRESSING

A delicious combination of strawberries and kiwi fruit harmonize well with the chicken to produce this colourful light salad.

☐ Very thinly slice the cooked chicken breast and fan out the slices on four plates. Arrange the kiwi fruit on the chicken slices.

☐ Arrange a few salad leaves at the 'point' of the fanned chicken.

☐ For the dressing, purée the strawberries. Whisk in the orange rind, olive oil and wine vinegar. Season to taste with salt and pepper. Spoon over the chicken slices.

☐ Garnish the salad with fresh strawberries and a sprinkling of coarsely crushed green peppercorns. Serve immediately.

CHICKEN WITH SEAFOOD SAUCE

An unusual combination of fowl and fish which tastes exceptionally good. Serve with a crisp green salad and new potatoes.

☐ Place the chicken in a large pan with the pared lemon rind, sliced onion, bayleaf and white wine. Add sufficient water to come halfway up the chicken.

☐ Chop 4 of the anchovy fillets and add them and the reserved prawn (shrimp) shells to the pan, season, cover and bring to the boil, then simmer for about 1½ hours or until the chicken is tender.

☐ Meanwhile, make the sauce. Blend together the mayonnaise, lemon juice, 1 tablespoonful of the capers and the drained tuna fish. When smooth, season with salt and pepper to taste.

☐ Remove the cooked chicken to a carving dish. Add sufficient of the strained cooking liquid to the tuna fish sauce to give a smooth, coating consistency.

☐ Carve the cooked chicken while still warm and arrange on a flat platter. Spoon the prepared sauce over the top. Chill. Garnish the chicken with the peeled prawns (shrimp), remaining anchovy fillets, capers and fresh basil.

SERVES 4

1 oven-ready chicken (about 1.5 kg/3½ lbs)
thinly pared rind of 1 lemon
1 small onion, thinly sliced
1 bayleaf
1¼ cups/300 ml/½ pt dry white wine
10 anchovy fillets
24 prawns (shrimp), peeled and shells reserved
salt and freshly ground black pepper
1¼ cups/300 ml/½ pt low calorie mayonnaise
juice of ½ lemon
30 ml/2 tbsp capers
200 g/7 oz can tuna fish in brine
fresh basil sprigs to garnish

SERVES 4

3 ripe peaches
1 ¼ cups/300 ml/½ pt dry white wine
2 strips lemon peel
15 ml/1 tbsp fresh tarragon, chopped
(or 2.5 ml/½ tsp dried)
salt and freshly ground black pepper
4 chicken breasts (approx. 150 g/5 oz each)
chicken stock (broth)
⅔ cup/150 ml/¼ pt fromage frais (preferably low fat)

GARNISH
Slices of skinned fresh peach (optional)
fresh tarragon sprigs

CHICKEN WITH PEACH AND TARRAGON SAUCE

Flavours of the summer enhance the chicken to make this an ideal meal to enjoy outdoors. Accompany it with a chilled green (stick or snap) bean salad and new potatoes.

☐ Make a nick in the stalk end of each peach and plunge them into a bowl of boiling water for about 40 seconds. Lift out with a slotted spoon and slip off the skins.

☐ Halve the peaches and discard the stones (pits). Chop the peach flesh roughly, and put in a pan with the wine, lemon peel, chopped tarragon and salt and pepper, to taste.

☐ Simmer gently for 10 minutes; cool slightly, then liquidize until smooth.

☐ Poach (or steam) the chicken breasts gently in the chicken stock until tender. Remove the skin and allow to cool.

☐ Mix the cooled peach purée with the fromage frais. If the sauce is too thick, add a little liquid from poaching the chicken. Adjust seasoning.

☐ Arrange the chicken breasts on a serving dish, spoon the peach sauce over the top and chill for an hour. To serve, garnish with slices of peach and sprigs of fresh tarragon.

CORONATION CHICKEN (BELOW LEFT)

This dish was developed by the Cordon Bleu Cookery School in London to celebrate the Queen's Coronation in 1953. It remains a firm favourite, particularly for buffets. Serve with a simple rice salad.

☐ Heat the oil, add the onion and cook for 3 to 4 minutes. Stir in the curry powder and cook for a further minute.

☐ Add the purée (paste), wine, water, bayleaf and lemon slices. Simmer, uncovered, for about 10 minutes or until well reduced. Strain and cool completely.

☐ Gradually beat the cooled sauce into the mayonnaise, then add the apricot jam (preserve) and fromage frais or yogurt. Adjust the seasoning.

☐ Lightly coat the chicken pieces with the mayonnaise. Pile onto a serving dish and garnish with a light dusting of paprika and thin slices of cucumber.

SERVES 6

1 × 2 kg/4 lb chicken, cooked and removed
from bones
15 ml/1 tbsp sunflower oil
1 small onion, finely chopped
10 ml/2 tsp curry powder
5 ml/1 tsp tomato purée (paste)
½ cup/125 ml/4 fl oz red wine
¼ cup/60 ml/4 tbsp water
1 bayleaf
2 slices lemon
¼ cup/60 ml/4 tbsp good quality apricot jam
(preserve)
1 ¼ cups/300 ml/½ pt low calorie mayonnaise
⅔ cup/150 ml/¼ pt fromage frais or natural yogurt
salt and freshly ground black pepper

GARNISH

paprika
cucumber slices

Coronation Chicken

Tomato Salad with Chicken Liver Dressing

TOMATO SALAD WITH CHICKEN LIVER DRESSING

A more unusual way of using chicken livers, but nonetheless delicious. Vary the salad by adding thickly sliced mushrooms or sliced onions. The dressing is also good served with plain cooked chicken.

☐ First prepare the tomatoes. Make an incision in the stem end of each, and plunge in boiling water for 40 seconds. Drain and slip off the skins. Slice thinly onto the serving plate, and sprinkle with the chopped spring onions (scallions). Chill.

☐ To make the dressing, heat 30 ml/2 tablespoonfuls of the oil. Sauté the livers with the chopped garlic until they just begin to brown.

☐ Spoon the livers and garlic into a food processor or liquidizer and blend together with the mustard, eggs and vinegar. Gradually drizzle in the remaining oil.

☐ Stir in the coarsely crushed peppercorns and season to taste. Spoon over the chilled tomatoes and serve immediately, garnished with a spring onion (scallion) curl and some snipped chives. Accompany with brown bread.

SERVES 4

4 beef tomatoes, peeled and thinly sliced
2 spring onions (scallions), trimmed and chopped
½ cup/125 ml/4 fl oz sunflower oil
5 chicken livers, washed, trimmed and chopped
1 clove garlic, finely chopped
5 ml/1 tsp wholegrain mustard
2 hard boiled (hard cooked) eggs
60 ml/4 tbsp wine vinegar
a few green peppercorns, crushed
salt, to taste

GARNISH

4 spring onion (scallion) curls (optional)
snipped fresh chives

SERVES 4

125 g/4 oz fresh spinach
4 boneless chicken breasts, skinned
(approx. 175 g/6 oz each)
50 g/2 oz smoked salmon slivers (or trimmings)
½ lemon, finely grated rind
salt and freshly ground black pepper
45 ml/3 tbsp sunflower oil
⅓ cup/90 ml/6 tbsp low calorie mayonnaise
15 ml/1 tbsp fresh dill, chopped
sprigs of dill

CHICKEN, SMOKED SALMON AND SPINACH ROULADE

These attractive 'pinwheels', accompanied by a dill mayonnaise and a crisp salad, are ideal for a summer lunch or picnic.

☐ Remove the thick stem part from each spinach leaf. Blanch spinach in boiling water for 1 minute, refresh in cold water and drain on absorbent paper (paper towel).

☐ Place each chicken breast between 2 sheets dampened greaseproof paper and flatten to approximately 1 cm/½ in thick, with a rolling pin. (Try to keep as neat a shape as possible.)

☐ Lay the drained spinach leaves over each chicken breast, smooth side down, then lay the smoked salmon on top and sprinkle over the grated lemon rind. Season to taste.

☐ Roll up, swiss roll (jelly roll) fashion, and secure with wooden cocktail sticks.

☐ Heat the oil in a shallow pan; add the chicken roulades and cook gently for 20 minutes, turning them occasionally until the chicken is tender.

☐ Allow to cool, then remove the cocktail sticks and wrap the cooked roulades in cling film (plastic wrap). Chill until required.

☐ To serve, slice the roulades and accompany with the mayonnaise, to which has been added the chopped dill, seasoned to taste. Garnish with dill sprigs.

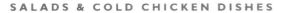

CHICKEN CHANTILLY

This is an ideal fork or buffet dish. It is very decorative and can be made in advance and assembled prior to serving.

- ☐ Put half the oil, the lemon juice, wine, stock, mushrooms, onions, tomato and bayleaf into a pan. Season well, bring to the boil, then simmer, covered, for 6 to 10 minutes.
- ☐ Heat the remaining oil in a pan and stir-fry the rice until it begins to go opaque.
- ☐ Strain off the liquor from the mushroom and onion, reserving the vegetables, and add enough boiling water or stock (broth) to make the quantity up to 2 cups/500 ml/18 fl oz. Pour this onto the rice, cover and cook until all the liquid is absorbed and the rice is just tender, about 20 to 25 minutes. Remove bayleaf, stir in the mushroom and onion and leave to cool.
- ☐ Arrange the rice mixture in a circle on a flat dish, leaving a hollow in the centre.
- ☐ Take the chicken meat off the bone and coarsely chop. Fold in the mayonnaise and fromage frais. Season to taste with salt and pepper. Pile on top of the rice pilaff.
- ☐ Garnish the top of the chicken with crosswise strips of pimento (sweet red pepper). Place the lettuce leaves in the centre of the dish, and sprinkle with the sieved egg yolk. Mix the chopped egg white with the parsley and spoon a thin line around the edge of the rice. Serve chilled.

SERVES 4 TO 6

30 ml/2 tbsp vegetable oil
juice of ½ lemon
⅓ cup/90 ml/6 tbsp white wine
3–4 pickling onions (or shallots), sliced
1 cup/125 g/4 oz button mushrooms, wiped and sliced
⅔ cup/150 ml/¼ pt chicken stock (broth) plus extra, if needed
1 tomato, peeled and deseeded
1 bayleaf
1½ cups/175 g/6 oz long grain rice
1 × 1.5 kg/3½ lb chicken, cooked
1¼ cups/300 ml/½ pt low calorie mayonnaise
⅔ cup/150 ml/¼ pt fromage frais
salt and freshly ground black pepper

GARNISH

1 hard boiled (hard cooked) egg (yolk sieved, egg white chopped)
1 lettuce heart
strips of canned pimento (sweet red pepper)
30 ml/2 tbsp fresh parsley, chopped

Mediterranean Chicken Salad

MEDITERRANEAN CHICKEN SALAD

Fresh herbs make all the difference in this summer salad. For a change, substitute the ham with flaked tuna fish, and the basil with fresh tarragon.

- ☐ Cut the chicken and ham into neat strips. Cut the beans into 2.5 cm/1 in lengths and the potatoes into small chunks. Place in a large bowl.
- ☐ Halve or slice the tomatoes, depending on size. Cut the cucumber in half lengthways, scoop out and discard the seeds, then cut the flesh into matchsticks. Add to the bowl.
- ☐ Fold these ingredients together carefully, together with the freshly chopped herbs and olives.
- ☐ In a screw top jar, shake together the olive oil, wine vinegar, lemon juice, mustard powder, cayenne, sugar and seasonings until well blended. Pour over the chicken salad.
- ☐ Spoon the salad into a glass serving dish. Garnish the top with fresh anchovies, and sprigs of fresh herbs. Chill for at least one hour before serving to allow the flavours to develop.

SERVES 6

175 g/6 oz cooked chicken
125 g/4 oz cooked ham
175 g/6 oz French beans or green (string or snap) beans, lightly cooked
175 g/6 oz new potatoes, cooked
4 plum or cherry tomatoes (yellow or red variety)
½ cucumber, peeled
12 black olives
15 ml/1 tbsp each freshly chopped basil, parsley and chives
¼ cup/60 ml/4 tbsp olive oil
15 ml/1 tbsp white wine vinegar
15 ml/1 tbsp lemon juice
pinch dry mustard powder
pinch cayenne
pinch caster (fine) sugar
salt and freshly ground black pepper
6 anchovies
fresh herb sprigs to garnish

SERVES 8

*hot water crust pastry made with 500 g/1 lb plain
(all purpose) flour (see page 13)*
750 g/1 ½ lb chicken breast, skinned and diced
500 g/1 lb gammon (raw smoked ham), diced
125 g/4 oz streaky bacon, derinded and diced
60 ml/4 tbsp chopped parsley
5 ml/1 tsp chopped thyme
5 ml/1 tsp green peppercorns, coarsely chopped
pinch grated nutmeg
¼ cup/60 ml/4 tbsp dry white wine
2 tbsp/25 g/1 oz butter
1 egg, beaten, to glaze
1 ¼ cups/300 ml/½ pt chicken stock (broth)
15 ml/1 tbsp powdered gelatine (gelatin)

*Oven temperature: 230 °C/450 °F/Gas 8, then
170° C/325 °F/Gas 3*

RAISED CHICKEN AND HAM PIE

A raised pie is a must for the traditional picnic hamper. It is easy to pack and carry and excellent accompanied with some cranberry or redcurrant jelly. Although special raised pie tins (pans) are available, in this case I prefer to use a deep loose-bottomed cake tin (pan).

☐ Lightly grease a deep 18 cm/7 inch cake tin (pan) with removable base. Roll out two thirds of the pastry to 6 mm/¼ inch thick. Line the cake tin (pan).

☐ In a bowl, mix together the chicken, gammon (ham), bacon, parsley, thyme, peppercorns and nutmeg. Spoon into the pastry case. Pour over the wine and dot with butter.

☐ Roll the remaining pastry into an 18 cm/7 in round. Brush the edges of the pie with some of the beaten egg. Cover with the circle of pastry and crimp the edges to seal.

☐ Glaze the top of the pie with more beaten egg. Cut a cross in the centre and lift up the pastry to form a small vent. Insert a small aluminium foil funnel into the hole.

☐ Re-roll the pastry trimmings and cut into leaves or tassles. Arrange on top of the pie. Glaze with the remaining beaten egg.

☐ Bake at the higher oven setting for 20 minutes, then reduce to the lower temperature and cook for 2 hours. Cover with aluminium foil to prevent the pastry from becoming too brown. Remove the foil 20 minutes before the end to crispen the pastry.

☐ Heat the stock (broth) in a saucepan. Sprinkle over the gelatine (gelatin) and stir over a gentle heat, until the gelatine has completely dissolved. Pour a little at a time through the funnel into the cooked pie.

☐ Cool the pie in the tin, then chill thoroughly. Turn out of the tin and serve.

LIGHT LUNCHES, SNACKS & SUPPERS

SICILIAN TOMATOES

Firm, round beef tomatoes are perfect for stuffing with the flavours of the Mediterranean, either as a starter or a supper dish. Try tuna fish as an alternative to chicken.

□ Slice the top off each tomato and scoop out the pulp and seeds; chop and reserve these for later use.

□ Heat the oil in a pan and gently cook the onion and garlic and pinenuts, until the onion is softened and the nuts golden brown.

□ Stir in the breadcrumbs and chicken. Cook for a further minute. Remove from the heat and stir in the oregano, capers, olives and salt and pepper to taste. Stir in the tomato pulp and add a dash of Tobasco sauce.

□ Spoon the stuffing mixture back into the tomato shells. Sprinkle with the Parmesan cheese.

□ Place the tomatoes on a greased baking tray and cook for 20 to 30 minutes or until tender and the Parmesan is golden. Serve warm.

SERVES 4 OR 8

8 beef tomatoes
30 ml/2 tbsp olive oil
1 medium onion, finely chopped
1 clove garlic, crushed (minced)
15 g/½ oz pinenuts
1 cup/50 g/2 oz fresh white breadcrumbs
175 g/6 oz cooked chicken, finely chopped or minced
30 ml/2 tbsp fresh oregano
10 ml/2 tsp capers, chopped
4 black olives, chopped
salt and pepper, freshly ground
dash Tobasco
25 g/1 oz Parmesan cheese, freshly grated

Oven temperature: 180 °C/350 °F/Gas 4

SERVES 4
GLAZE
30 ml/2 tbsp white wine
grated rind 1 orange
⅓ cup/90 ml/6 tbsp orange juice
15 ml/1 tbsp lemon juice
75 ml/5 tbsp honey or stem ginger syrup
2.5 ml/½ tsp ground cinnamon
5 ml/1 tsp ground ginger
5 ml/1 tsp black peppercorns, crushed
5 ml/1 tsp coriander seeds, crushed
12 fresh chicken wings
GARNISH
rind of 1 orange, julienned (see Glossary, p93)
fresh orange segments
fresh mint

Oven temperature: 190 °C/375 °F/Gas 5

ORANGE GLAZED CHICKEN WINGS

- Mix all the glaze ingredients together in a large bowl. Add the chicken wings, cover and marinade for at least 4 hours, preferably overnight, in the refrigerator.
- Line a small roasting tin with a double layer of foil. Pour in the chicken wings and glaze. Arrange the wings so they are outer side uppermost.
- Bake for 50 to 60 minutes, basting regularly with the glaze. If the glaze is still quite liquid at the end of the cooking time, pour it off into a small pan and boil rapidly until it reduces and thickens. Spoon this back over the wings.
- Serve the chicken wings hot or cold, garnished with julienne strips of orange rind, orange segments, and fresh mint.

Chicken Thighs with Lemon and Pepper

Orange Glazed Chicken Wings

CHICKEN THIGHS WITH LEMON AND PEPPER

A simple and quickly prepared chicken dish to cook over the barbecue.

- With a zester, remove the peel from 1 lemon or grate finely so that only the yellow part is removed. Squeeze the juice from both lemons and put into a dish with the peel, garlic, oil, black pepper, and salt to season.
- Add the chicken thighs, cover and marinate for at least 4 to 6 hours, preferably overnight.
- Cook on a hot barbecue for 15 to 20 minutes, turning halfway through and brushing with the marinade.

SERVES 4
2 lemons
2 cloves garlic, finely chopped
30 ml/2 tbsp olive oil
10 ml/2 tsp coarsely ground black pepper
salt
8 chicken thighs

Red Legged Chicken

RED LEGGED CHICKEN

Delicious hot or cold and perfect for a picnic, prepare these drumsticks well in advance for barbecuing, grilling, or roasting.

☐ With a sharp knife, make 2 or 3 small incisions in each chicken drumstick.

☐ Put the sweet (bell) pepper under a hot grill (broiler) and cook until the skin is blistered all over. Place in a polythene bag and leave to 'sweat' for 10 minutes.

☐ Remove the skin and seeds from the pepper, chop roughly, and blend in a food processor or liquidizer, together with the remaining ingredients.

☐ Pour the purée into a shallow dish, add the chicken drumsticks and turn them thoroughly in the purée to coat evenly. Cover and chill for at least 4 hours or preferably overnight, to allow the flavours to be absorbed.

☐ Either cook the drumsticks over hot barbecue coals, grill (broil), or transfer to a roasting tin (pan) and cook in a preheated oven for 35 to 40 minutes or until tender.

SERVES 4

8 chicken drumsticks
1 large sweet red (bell) pepper
5 ml/1 tsp paprika
2.5 ml/½ tsp Cayenne
15 ml/1 tbsp lemon juice
30 ml/2 tbsp sunflower oil
1 clove garlic, crushed (minced)
salt

Oven temperature: 200 °C/400 °F/Gas 6

SERVES 4 OR 8

8 large flat mushrooms
15 ml/1 tbsp sunflower oil plus a little extra
1 small onion, finely chopped
1 clove garlic, finely chopped
25 g/4 oz boneless chicken (thigh or breast)
2 rashers lean smoked bacon, derinded
2 cups/125 g/4 oz fresh white breadcrumbs
15 ml/1 tbsp Worcestershire sauce
good pinch mustard powder
salt and freshly ground black pepper
1 egg, beaten
40 g/1 ½ oz Parmesan cheese, freshly grated
30 ml/2 tbsp milk
freshly chopped parsley to garnish

Oven temperature: 200 °C/400 °F/Gas 6

Country Mushrooms

COUNTRY MUSHROOMS

Large open field mushrooms are full of flavour on their own, but are also good topped with this savoury stuffing for a starter or light meal. Chicken livers could be used instead of chicken.

☐ Remove the stalks from the mushrooms and chop finely.
☐ Heat the oil in a pan, and sauté the onions and garlic until softened. Add the chopped mushroom stalks and cook for a further minute.
☐ Finely dice the chicken and bacon and add to the pan. Stir-fry for a further 2 minutes. Remove from the heat and mix in the breadcrumbs, Worcestershire sauce, mustard and seasonings. Stir in the beaten egg.
☐ Spoon the mixture into the mushroom caps to form neat mounds.
☐ Drizzle a small amount of oil over the top of each filled mushroom and then sprinkle with a little Parmesan cheese.
☐ Place the mushrooms on a large, lightly oiled baking tray (cookie sheet). Add the milk to prevent the mushrooms from drying out.
☐ Bake for 20 minutes. Serve hot, sprinkled liberally with chopped parsley.

Chicken and Avocado Quiche

SERVES 6

250 g/8 oz shortcrust pastry
1 small onion, finely chopped
15 ml/1 tbsp sunflower oil
250 g/8 oz cooked chicken, finely chopped
1 firm avocado pear, peeled, stoned (pitted) and cubed
75 g/3 oz low fat cream cheese, cut into small knobs
15 ml/1 tbsp each freshly chopped tarragon, parsley and chives
3 eggs
scant cup/200 ml/7 fl oz milk
salt and freshly ground black pepper

GARNISH
thin slivers of peeled avocado dipped in lemon juice
chopped parsley or chives

Oven temperature: 190 °C/375 °F/Gas 5

CHICKEN AND AVOCADO QUICHE

Try the subtle combination of chicken, avocado and cream cheese. Courgettes (zucchini) sliced and blanched make a good alternative to avocado if you prefer.

☐ Roll out the pastry fairly thinly and use to line a 23 cm/9 in diameter loose-bottomed fluted flan ring. Place on a baking sheet (cookie sheet). Fill with a circle of greaseproof paper and baking beans. Bake 'blind' for 10 to 15 minutes.
☐ Cook the onion gently in the oil for 3 to 4 minutes. Scatter over the base of the pastry case. Add the chicken, avocado, cream cheese and herbs.
☐ Beat together the eggs, milk and seasoning, to taste. Pour into the pastry case. Cook for 35 minutes or until the filling is set.
☐ Serve either warm or cold, garnished with slices of avocado and freshly chopped herbs.

BAKED STUFFED SWEET (BELL) PEPPERS

When buying the sweet (bell) peppers, choose squat round peppers which still stand upright. Choose green, red, yellow or orange peppers, or even a mixture. Serve accompanied with a bowl of hot Fresh Tomato Sauce (see page 60).

☐ Cut the tops off the peppers and remove the cores and seeds. Put the peppers in a basin, cover with boiling water and allow to stand for 5 minutes. Drain thoroughly and set aside.

☐ Heat half the oil in a large pan and sauté the onion until softened. Stir in the rice and mushrooms and cook for a further minute; add the stock (broth), bring to the boil and simmer, covered, for 15 minutes, until the rice is just tender and the stock absorbed.

☐ Stir in the tomato purée (paste) and the freshly chopped basil. Season to taste.

☐ Heat the remaining oil and sauté the chicken livers until lightly browned. Stir into the rice with the pinenuts.

☐ Spoon the rice mixture into the peppers and sprinkle them with the cheese.

☐ Arrange the peppers in an ovenproof dish. Pour a little water into the dish (just enough to cover its base) and cook for 35 minutes or until the peppers are tender. Serve hot, garnished with fresh basil leaves.

SERVES 4

4 even-sized sweet (bell) peppers
30 ml/2 tbsp sunflower oil
I small onion, finely chopped
I cup/125 g/4 oz long grain rice
¼ cup/50 g/2 oz button mushrooms, chopped
2 cups/450 ml/¾ pt chicken stock (broth)
¼ cup/60 ml/4 tbsp tomato purée (paste)
30 ml/2 tbsp fresh basil, chopped
salt and freshly ground black pepper
4–6 chicken livers, chopped
30 ml/2 tbsp pinenuts, toasted
30 ml/2 tbsp finely grated Parmesan cheese
fresh basil leaves to garnish

Oven temperature: 180 °C/350 °F/Gas 4

CHICKEN NUGGETS

MAKES APPROX 18

500 g/1 lb boneless chicken, minced
1 cup/50 g/2 oz fresh white breadcrumbs
¼ cup/60 ml/4 tbsp mango chutney
1 small onion, finely chopped
5 ml/1 tsp ground coriander, (cilantro)
salt and freshly ground black pepper
1 egg, lightly beaten
30 ml/2 tbsp wholemeal flour
30 ml/2 tbsp vegetable oil

Good enough on their own as a cocktail snack, or served with a relish and salad. For a more substantial 'nugget', replace breadcrumbs with cooked rice.

- ☐ In a large bowl, combine the chicken, breadcrumbs, chutney, onion, coriander and seasonings. Add enough beaten egg to bind the ingredients together.
- ☐ Shape the mixture into small 'nuggets' the size of a cork. Dust lightly with the wholemeal flour.
- ☐ Heat the oil in a large frying pan (skillet) and cook the 'nuggets' for 10 to 15 minutes, turning frequently, until golden brown. Serve hot or cold.

Chicken Nuggets

Crunchy Nut Drumsticks

CHICKEN STUFFED POTATO BAKES

SERVES 4

4 large baking potatoes, wiped
30 ml/2 tbsp sunflower oil
1 small leek, trimmed and thinly sliced
3 rashers streaky bacon, derinded and chopped
250 g/8 oz boned chicken breast, skinned and chopped
⅓ cup/50 g/2 oz button mushrooms, chopped
salt and freshly ground black pepper
2.5 ml/½ tsp ground nutmeg
¼ cup/60 ml/4 tbsp fromage frais
30 ml/2 tbsp milk
1 egg yolk
30 ml/2 tbsp parsley or chives, chopped
40 g/1 ½ oz Parmesan cheese, freshly grated

Oven temperature: 190 °C/375 °F/Gas 5

These jacket potatoes make a tasty and simply prepared winter supper dish. They can be made well in advance, chilled and then heated through when required. Vary the ingredients to suit the contents of your store cupboard or fridge!

- ☐ Bake the potatoes for 1½ hours or until tender. Leave to cool slightly, halve lengthways, and carefully scoop the cooked potato out into a bowl. Reserve the intact skins.
- ☐ Heat the oil in a pan and fry the leeks and bacon until the leeks soften and the bacon is crisp. Add the diced chicken and mushrooms. Season, and stir-fry for 4 to 5 minutes or until the chicken is tender. Sprinkle on the nutmeg.
- ☐ Either mash or purée the potato together with the fromage frais, milk and egg yolk. When smooth, stir in the chicken mixture and the chopped parsley. Adjust the seasoning, if necessary.
- ☐ Pile the potato mixture back into the shells. Sprinkle with the Parmesan cheese, and heat through for 20 minutes or until slightly risen and golden brown. Serve immediately.

CRUNCHY NUT DRUMSTICKS

Children and adults alike will enjoy these crunchy drumsticks, especially when partnered with contrasting dips.

☐ Mix together the breadcrumbs, peanuts, parsley, garlic granules, curry powder and paprika.

☐ Dip the drumsticks into the beaten egg, drain well, then coat with the breadcrumb mixture.

☐ Place the drumsticks in a large shallow roasting tin. Drizzle over the peanut oil, and then cook for 40 minutes until golden brown and crisp.

☐ Meanwhile make the dips. For the Mexican Dip, simmer the onion and vinegar in a small pan for 5 minutes. Stir in the remaining ingredients. Simmer for a couple of minutes more. Season to taste. Serve garnished with finely sliced spring onion.

☐ For the Avocado Dip, put all the ingredients, except for the paprika, in a food processor or liquidizer and blend until smooth. Season to taste. Serve sprinkled with paprika.

Lentil and Chicken Loaf

LENTIL AND CHICKEN LOAF

Serve this loaf hot or cold, accompanied with your favourite fresh tomato sauce.

☐ Soak the lentils in cold water overnight. Drain, and put in a pan with sufficient cold water to cover. Add the sprig of sage, the small onion with cloves and the garlic. Bring to the boil, then cover and cook for 25 to 30 minutes or until the lentils are tender. Drain, discarding the sage and the onion.

☐ Mix the cooked lentils with the chopped onion, cheese, yogurt, eggs, chopped sage, chicken and season to taste.

☐ Pour into a greased and base-lined 1 kg/2 lb loaf tin (pan), and smooth the surface level. Cook for 1 hour. Allow to cool in the tin for 10 minutes before turning out. Cut into slices to serve.

MAKES 12

2 cups/125 g/4 oz fresh white breadcrumbs
¼ cup/60 ml/4 tbsp salted peanuts, finely chopped
30 ml/2 tbsp parsley, chopped
5 ml/1 tsp dried garlic granules
2.5 ml/½ tsp curry powder
2.5 ml/½ tsp paprika
12 chicken drumsticks
2 eggs, beaten
45 ml/3 tbsp peanut oil

MEXICAN DIP

45 ml/3 tbsp grated onion
45 ml/3 tbsp white wine vinegar
⅔ cup/150 ml/¼ pt tomato ketchup
5 ml/1 tsp Worcestershire sauce
juice of ½ lemon
2.5 ml/½ tsp paprika
salt
1 spring onion (scallion), trimmed and
finely sliced

AVOCADO DIP

1 ripe avocado, peeled and stoned (pitted)
15 ml/1 tbsp lemon juice
⅔ cup/150 ml/¼ pt low calorie mayonnaise
dash Tabasco
salt
paprika

Oven temperature: 180 °C/350 °F/Gas 4

SERVES 6

250 g/8 oz lentils
1 sprig fresh sage
1 small onion, studded with 4 cloves
1 clove garlic, crushed (minced)
1 medium onion, finely chopped
75 g/3 oz cheddar cheese, grated
⅔ cup/150 ml/¼ pt low fat yogurt
2 eggs, beaten
15 ml/1 tbsp fresh sage, chopped
175 g/6 oz cooked chicken, finely chopped
salt and freshly ground black pepper

Oven temperature: 180 °C/350 °F/Gas 4

PASTA & RICE DISHES

SERVES 4 TO 6

500 g/1 lb boneless chicken breast, skinned and cubed
30 ml/2 tbsp sunflower oil
1 onion, finely sliced
2 cloves garlic, crushed (minced)
5 ml/1 tsp dried oregano
2 cups/250 g/8 oz Arborio or long grain rice
15 ml/1 tbsp tomato purée (paste)
5 cups/1.2 l/2 pt strong chicken stock (broth),
(see page 11)
splash dry white wine
salt and freshly ground black pepper
6 tomatoes, skinned, deseeded and chopped
10 pitted black olives, halved
30 ml/2 oz Parmesan cheese, grated

CHICKEN RISOTTO

A true Italian risotto uses Arborio rice, which contributes to the characteristic creamy texture. If you prefer a slightly 'wetter' risotto, add a little more stock (or wine!).

☐ Heat the oil in a large pan, and cook the onion and garlic over a gentle heat until softened. Add the chicken and cook until golden brown.

☐ Add the oregano and rice and cook for a further minute, stirring well. Blend in the tomato purée (paste), stock (broth) and wine. Season to taste and stir well.

☐ Cook over a gentle heat for 25 to 30 minutes or until all the liquid has been absorbed, but the rice still has a nutty bite to it.

☐ Lightly fork in the tomatoes, olives and chopped parsley or basil. Heat through for a further 2 minutes. Serve, sprinkled with the Parmesan cheese.

CHICKEN, MUSHROOM AND SPINACH LASAGNE

A tasty lasagne, accompanied with a crisp salad and crusty brown bread makes for easy and informal entertaining. Prepare the lasagne in advance and chill until you are ready to cook it.

☐ To make the chicken sauce, heat the oil in a pan and cook the onion gently until softened. Add the diced chicken and stir-fry until the chicken is firm and cooked through.

☐ In another saucepan, melt the butter. Add the flour and cook, stirring, for one minute. Remove from the heat and slowly blend in the milk, beating to a smooth sauce between each addition. Return to the heat and bring to the boil and cook for one minute. Season with the nutmeg, salt and pepper.

☐ Put a third of the sauce into a bowl and reserve. Add the chicken and onion mixture to the remaining sauce. Place a layer of damp grease-proof paper on the surface of both sauces to prevent a skin forming.

☐ For the mushroom and spinach mixture, heat the oil and cook the onion and garlic gently until softened. Add the mushrooms and cook gently for 10 minutes or until any liquid has evaporated.

☐ Cook the spinach briefly in a large covered saucepan until it has wilted (see Glossary, page 93) and reduced in volume. No need to add any water. Drain, squeeze out any excess liquid and then chop finely. Add to the mushroom mixture and season to taste.

☐ Lightly oil a deep rectangular ovenproof dish approx. 30 × 18 cm (12 × 7 in). Line the bottom and sides of the dish with some of the pasta and then layer with half the chicken sauce, pasta, spinach and mushroom sauce, more pasta, the remaining chicken sauce, pasta and the plain sauce.

☐ Sprinkle with the grated Parmesan and cook for 45 to 50 minutes or until bubbling and golden brown on top.

SERVES 6

CHICKEN & NUTMEG SAUCE
15 ml/1 tbsp sunflower oil
1 small onion, finely chopped
500 g/1 lb uncooked chicken meat, cut into 1 cm (½ in) cubes
½ cup/125 g/4 oz butter
scant cup/125 g/4 oz plain (all purpose) flour
3¾ cups/900 ml/1 ½ pt semi-skimmed milk
2.5 ml/½ tsp freshly grated nutmeg
salt and freshly ground black pepper

MUSHROOM & SPINACH MIXTURE
15 ml/1 tbsp sunflower oil
1 onion, finely chopped
3 cloves garlic, crushed (minced)
375 g/12 oz flat mushrooms, finely chopped
375 g/12 oz fresh spinach, washed
salt and freshly ground black pepper

300–375 g/10–12 oz green pre-cooked lasagne (approximately 12 sheets)
50 g/2 oz Parmesan cheese, freshly grated

Oven temperature: 190 °C/375 °F/Gas 5

SERVES 8

1 × 1½ kg/3½ lb roasting chicken with giblets
⅓ cup/90 ml/6 tbsp sunflower oil
250 g/8 oz squid, cleaned and chopped
2 large onions, chopped
2 large cloves garlic, chopped
250 g/8 oz tomatoes, skinned, seeded and chopped
1 bayleaf
1 sprig fresh thyme
200 g/7 oz live mussels, scrubbed and debearded
200 g/7 oz chorizo or other spicy sausage, cut into chunks
500 g/1 lb Valencia or best risotto rice
175 g/6 oz shelled prawns (shrimp)
250 g/8 oz monkfish, cubed
1 sweet green (bell) pepper and
1 sweet red (bell) pepper, seeded and cut into
1 cm/1 in pieces
175 g/6 oz small French or green (string or snap) beans, top and tailed
75 g/3 oz frozen peas (or 250 g/8 oz peas in pod)
50 g/2 oz mange tout, top and tailed
15 saffron strands, soaked in 30 ml/2 tbsp hot water
10 ml/2 tsp paprika
salt

GARNISH

2 lemons
freshly chopped parsley
8 unshelled prawns (shrimp)

PAELLA VALENCIANA

'Paella' is a traditional Spanish speciality, shared at celebrations and among friends. There are many local variations, but the essential ingredients are rice and saffron, with a choice of chicken, shellfish and vegetables. The word 'paella' refers to the huge round shallow pan or 'paelleras' this dish is cooked in, and because these pans could measure anything from 30 cm (12 in) to a metre (3 ft) across, they are usually placed on an open fire for cooking.

- ☐ Joint the chicken, and then carefully chop into 5 cm/2 inch squares, keeping the meat on the bones.
- ☐ Place the carcass, together with the giblets and 3 cups/170 ml/1¼ pints water, in a pan. Add any fish skin and bones and the herbs together with a little salt and pepper.
- ☐ In a large pan, heat 30 ml/2 tablespoonfuls of the oil and brown the chicken all over, for about 10 minutes. Add the squid, cover and simmer for 10 minutes.
- ☐ Add the onion and garlic and cook until soft and just turning golden.
- ☐ Add the tomatoes. Simmer the mixture, uncovered, until the tomatoes have reduced to a pulp. This will take about 10 minutes.
- ☐ Add the mussels and chorizo or sausage. Cover and cook for 2 to 3 minutes or until the mussels have opened. Remove the pan from the heat.
- ☐ Heat the remaining oil in a paella pan or large frying pan (skillet). When the oil is hot, add the rice and cook, stirring, for 3 to 4 minutes.
- ☐ Add the chicken mixture to the rice, together with the prawns, monkfish, peppers, beans, peas and mange tout, saffron (plus soaking liquid), paprika and salt. Cook, stirring, for 2 minutes.
- ☐ Pour on 2¼ cups/500 ml/18 fl oz of the strained stock. Bring to the boil, then reduce the heat immediately to a gentle simmer.
- ☐ Cook for 15 to 20 minutes, shaking the pan from time to time (do not stir), and adding a little more stock if the mixture is drying out.
- ☐ Five minutes before the end, add the unshelled prawns (shrimp).
- ☐ Garnish the paella with lemon wedges and freshly chopped parsley, and serve from the pan, accompanied with some good Spanish wine.

CHICKEN BIRYANI

Traditionally, Biryanis are served at Indian or Persian banquets and feasts and require little more than a yogurt and cucumber relish or a simple vegetable accompaniment. Partially cooked, saffron scented rice is laid over the spicy chicken and baked in a very slow oven. Allow yourself plenty of time for preparation.

- ☐ Rinse the rice under cold running water until the water runs clear. Then leave to soak in a bowl of cold water for 30 minutes.
- ☐ Cut the chicken into bite sized pieces.
- ☐ Soak the saffron threads in the milk and boiling water for at least 15 minutes.
- ☐ Put the yogurt in a bowl and fold in the chicken together with the salt. Leave aside for 20 minutes.
- ☐ In a liquidizer or processor, blend a quarter of the sliced onions, the ginger, garlic and half the almonds, with 45 ml/3 tbsp water to form a thick paste.
- ☐ In a large ovenproof dish, heat two thirds of the oil. Add the remaining onion slices and cook until crisp and golden brown. Remove with a slotted spoon.
- ☐ Add the rest of the almonds and cook until browned. Remove and set aside for a garnish.
- ☐ Add the remaining oil to the pan and when hot, add the drained chicken pieces, a few at a time. Remove the pieces from the pan, as they become browned. Once all the chicken is done, add the garlicky paste to the pan and cook for a few minutes. Return the chicken to the pan, together with the onions, yogurt and ⅔ cup/150 ml/¼ pt water. Simmer, covered, for 20 minutes.
- ☐ Meanwhile, grind together the peppercorns, cardamom, coriander and cumin seeds. Blend together with the crumbled cinnamon stick, nutmeg and cayenne.
- ☐ Remove the lid from the chicken. Stir in the coarsely ground spices and cook, uncovered, for a further 10 minutes or until the sauce has thickened.
- ☐ Parboil the rice in a large saucepan of salted water. Boil rapidly for 6 minutes only. Drain.
- ☐ Pile the rice on top of the chicken. Drizzle on the saffron and its liquid. Cover tightly with foil, and a lid. Bake for 1 hour, or until the rice is tender.
- ☐ To serve, mix the contents of the pan gently. Serve on a warmed platter, garnished with the eggs, the browned almonds and coriander sprigs.

SERVES 6 TO 8

6 cups/750 g/1 ½ lb long grain or basmati rice
1 kg/2 lb boneless chicken (thigh and breast) skinned
5 ml/1 tsp saffron threads
45 ml/3 tbsp milk
30 ml/2 tbsp boiling water
1 ¼ cups/300 ml/½ pt natural yogurt
10 ml/2 tsp salt
2 large onions, peeled, halved and sliced
2.5 cm/1 in fresh ginger
3 cloves garlic
¼ cup/60 ml/4 tbsp blanched slivered almonds
⅓ cup/90 ml/6 tbsp vegetable oil
4 cloves
2.5 ml/½ tsp black peppercorns
2.5 ml/½ tsp cardamom seeds
2.5 ml/½ tsp coriander (cilantro) seeds
2.5 ml/½ tsp cumin seeds
5 cm/2 in stick cinnamon
2 pinches grated nutmeg
2 pinches cayenne pepper
salt

GARNISH
3 hard boiled (hard cooked) eggs, sliced
fresh coriander (cilantro) sprigs

Oven temperature: 150 °C/300 °F/Gas 2

SERVES 4

15 ml/1 tbsp sunflower oil
8 chicken thighs
1 large onion, sliced
5 ml/1 tsp paprika
5 ml/1 tsp ground cumin
5 ml/1 tsp turmeric
2.5 ml/½ tsp dried thyme
freshly ground black pepper
1 ¼ cups/300 ml/½ pt well flavoured chicken stock
(broth) (see page 11)
25 g/1 oz pitted black olives
30 ml/2 tbsp fresh coriander (cilantro), finely chopped
squeeze lemon juice

PILAU RICE

30 ml/2 tbsp vegetable oil
¼ cup/50 g/2 oz whole blanched almonds, toasted
1 small onion, finely diced
¼ cup/50 g/2 oz sultanas or raisins
3 cups/375 g/12 oz long grain rice
3¼ cups/750 ml/1 ¼ pt boiling water
2.5 ml/½ tsp salt

CORIANDER (CILANTRO) CHICKEN WITH PILAU RICE

Fresh coriander (cilantro) has a unique, pungent flavour.

☐ Heat the oil in a large pan and fry the chicken until an even, rich brown. Transfer to a plate.

☐ Add the onion to the remaining oil and cook until softened and golden. Stir in the paprika, cumin and turmeric and cook for a further minute. Add the thyme, black pepper and stock and bring to the boil.

☐ Return the chicken to the pan, skin side down. Cover and simmer for 1 to 1¼ hours or until the chicken is tender.

☐ Remove the chicken with a slotted spoon to a heated serving dish and keep warm.

☐ Reduce the sauce by rapidly boiling until it thickens. Stir in the olives, coriander (cilantro) and lemon juice. Season to taste and pour over the chicken.

☐ For the rice, heat the oil in a large pan and cook the onion until softened but not coloured. Add the toasted almonds, sultanas and rice, and cook for a further minute, stirring thoroughly.

☐ Add the boiling water and salt. Bring to the boil, then cover and reduce the heat to a simmer. Cook for 15 minutes, or until all the water has been absorbed and the rice is tender, but still firm. Fork the rice lightly and serve with the chicken.

SERVES 4

250 g/8 oz dried pasta shapes
30 ml/2 tbsp vegetable oil
250 g/8 oz chicken livers, cleaned and sliced
50 g/2 oz lean bacon, derinded and chopped
2 small courgettes (zucchini), sliced
4 spring onions (scallions), trimmed and sliced
1 cup/125 g/4 oz button mushrooms, sliced
1 small sweet red (bell) pepper, halved and cut into strips
30 ml/2 tbsp redcurrant jelly
⅔ cup/150 ml/¼ pt dry white wine or chicken stock (broth)
10 ml/2 tsp freshly chopped sage
¼ cup/60 ml/4 tbsp natural yogurt or fromage frais
salt and freshly ground black pepper
freshly chopped parsley to garnish

SPEEDY CHICKEN LIVERS WITH PASTA

This chicken liver dish makes an all-in-one lunch or supper dish. If you do not wish to use pasta, serve the chicken livers on a bed of boiled brown rice.

☐ Cook the pasta in boiling salted water until 'al dente'.

☐ Meanwhile heat the oil in a pan and add the chicken livers and bacon and stir-fry for 1 minute. Add the courgettes (zucchini), spring onion (scallions), mushrooms and peppers and cook for a further 2 minutes.

☐ Stir in the redcurrant jelly, wine or stock, sage and salt and pepper. Cover and simmer for 4 to 5 minutes.

☐ Drain the pasta. Fold the chicken livers together with the yogurt or fromage frais.

☐ Sprinkle thickly with chopped parsley and serve immediately.

Coriander (Cilantro) Chicken with Pilau Rice

SERVES 4 TO 6

2 cups/250 g/8 oz long grain rice
¼ cup/60 ml/4 tbsp groundnut oil
2 onions, finely chopped
I clove garlic, finely chopped
I fresh red chilli (chili), finely shredded
2 tomatoes, skinned, seeded and chopped
250 g/8 oz cooked chicken, diced
75 g/6 oz cooked prawns (shrimp), coarsely chopped
salt and freshly ground black pepper
30 ml/2 tbsp chopped fresh coriander (cilantro)

OMELETTE

15 ml/1 tbsp groundnut oil
3 spring onions (scallions) finely chopped
salt and freshly ground black pepper
30 ml/2 tbsp light soy sauce
4 eggs, beaten

GARNISH

paprika
cucumber slices

NASIGORENG

This dish originates from Malaysia, and makes good use of any left-over cooked meat, fish and vegetables. It is quick to prepare and makes the perfect informal fork supper dish.

☐ Cook the rice until just tender. Drain thoroughly and spread out on a tray to cool.

☐ Heat the oil in a large pan. Sauté the onions and garlic until softened and golden. Add the chilli (chili) and cook for a further 2 minutes.

☐ Stir in the tomatoes, chicken and prawns (shrimp). Cook for 2 minutes, then add the rice. Stir-fry until the rice turns a light golden colour. Season to taste. Stir in the fresh coriander (cilantro).

☐ Mound the rice mixture onto a platter, cover and keep warm.

☐ For the omelette, heat the oil in a large frying pan. Add the spring onions (scallions) and cook until softened.

☐ Season with salt and pepper and add the soy sauce. Cook for a further 2 minutes.

☐ Stir the beaten eggs into the pan. Cook over a low heat until the omelette is set.

☐ Carefully remove the omelette from the pan onto a chopping board. Loosely roll and shred it finely.

☐ Arrange the shreds of omelette over the rice. Sprinkle with a light dusting of paprika and garnish with cucumber slices. Serve immediately, with extra soy sauce and a selection of salads and relishes.

ORIENTAL, HOT & SPICY

CHICKEN WITH SPRING ONIONS (SCALLIONS) AND CASHEW NUTS

The dish is typical of many Chinese recipes – full of flavour, contrasting textures and colours and quickly prepared. Stir-frying ensures that the chicken juices are sealed in and very little goodness, nutritionally, is lost during cooking.

- ☐ Cut the chicken into 1 cm/½ inch cubes. Place in a bowl with the egg white, salt and 15 ml/1 tbsp sherry and mix well.
- ☐ Heat the oil in a large frying pan (skillet) or wok, and stir-fry the chicken for 2 minutes. Transfer to absorbent kitchen paper to drain.
- ☐ Pour off the oil, wipe the pan clean and return 15 ml/1 tbsp oil to the pan.
- ☐ Add the cashews, mushrooms, water chestnuts and half the spring onions (scallions) to the hot oil. Stir-fry for 1 minute, then add the soy sauce and the rest of the sherry.
- ☐ Return the chicken to the pan and stir-fry for another 2 minutes.
- ☐ Serve immediately, sprinkled with the remaining spring onions (scallions) and garnished with spring onion (scallion) tassles or curls if desired.

NOTE
If Chinese mushrooms are used, first soak them for 15 minutes in warm water.

SERVES 4

375 g/12 oz boneless chicken breasts, skinned
1 egg white
5 ml/1 tsp cornflour (cornstarch)
5 ml/1 tsp salt
45 ml/3 tbsp dry sherry
⅓ cup/90 ml/6 tbsp groundnut oil
¼ cup/50 g/2 oz cashew nuts
½ cup/50 g/2 oz mushrooms, sliced (see Note below)
50 g/2 oz water chestnuts, halved
4 large spring onions (scallions), trimmed and sliced into 2.5 cm/1 in lengths
15 ml/1 tbsp soy sauce
4 spring onion tassles or curls to garnish (optional)

SERVES 4
SAUCE
20 ml/4 tsp cornflour (cornstarch)
juice and rind 1 lemon
30 ml/2 tbsp clear honey
5 ml/1 tsp stem ginger, finely chopped
10 ml/2 tsp stem ginger syrup
10 ml/2 tsp sesame oil
10 ml-2 tsp light soy sauce
1 ½ cups/375 ml/12 fl oz (boiling) chicken stock (broth)
salt and freshly ground black pepper

CHICKEN
750 g/1 ½ lb boneless chicken breast, skinned
15 ml/1 tbsp cornflour (cornstarch)
grated rind ½ lemon
30 ml/2 tbsp groundnut oil
freshly ground black pepper

GARNISH
2 spring onions (scallions), trimmed and finely chopped
or snipped fresh chives
julienne of lemon peel (see Glossary, p93)

LEMON CHICKEN CHINESE STYLE

The combination of lemon and chicken has been used in many good recipes and this one is no exception. It is quickly prepared and cooked and delicious accompanied with brown rice.

☐ First make the sauce. In a pan blend the cornflour (cornstarch) with the lemon juice and rind to make a smooth paste. Stir in the honey, ginger, syrup and oil and soy sauce. Pour on the boiling stock (broth) and bring to the boil, stirring, until thickened. Season to taste with salt and pepper. Simmer gently for 10 minutes.

☐ Cut the chicken into 2.5 cm/1 in strips. Place in a bowl, and sprinkle with the cornflour, lemon rind and plenty of ground black pepper.

☐ Heat the oil in a non-stick frying pan. Add the chicken pieces and stir-fry for 10 minutes or until the chicken is golden brown and tender.

☐ Transfer the chicken to a warm serving plate. Spoon over the lemon sauce and garnish with finely chopped spring onions (scallions) or chives and julienne of lemon peel. Serve immediately.

CHINESE MONEY BAGS

These small pouches of seasoned minced meats are a familiar snack in the tea-houses of Southern China – and are also known as dim sum or steamed open dumplings. Very 'moreish', and delicious eaten on their own or with a 'dunking' sauce such as a proprietary Chinese plum sauce. I have included a simple recipe for making your own dough; alternatively good Chinese grocers sell fresh or frozen 'wuntun skins'.

- ☐ Sift the flour and salt into a bowl. Add the egg yolk and nearly all the water to mix to a dough. Knead on a floured surface until the dough is smooth and pliable. Only add extra water if required. Place the dough back in the bowl, cover and leave to rest for 30 minutes.
- ☐ Put all the ingredients for the filling in a bowl and mix together well.
- ☐ Knead the dough once more and then cut into 18 pieces. Roll each piece into a ball using lightly floured hands, and then roll it out to a 7.5 cm (3 in) diameter circle.
- ☐ Place a heaped teaspoonful of the mixture in the centre of each circle. Gather the dough up around the filling, pinching the sides into a 'gathered pouch'. Leave the top open.
- ☐ Place the dumplings in a steaming basket and steam in a covered pan for 20 minutes. Keep each batch warm, in a low oven, covered in foil until all the money bags are ready.

NOTE

Filled 'money bags' can be frozen successfully and thawed when required. Likewise, the dish can be made and cooked ahead of time and then briefly re-steamed when you are ready to serve.

MAKES 18

DOUGH

I cup/125 g/4 oz plain (all purpose) flour, plus extra for dusting
pinch salt
I egg yolk
½ cup/125 ml/4 fl oz hot water

FILLING

175 g/6 oz minced chicken
75 g/3 oz peeled prawns (shrimp), chopped
25 g/1 oz parma ham, chopped
15 ml/1 tbsp light soy sauce
10 ml/2 tsp dry sherry or rice wine
3 spring onions (scallions), trimmed and chopped finely
15 ml/1 tsp fresh ginger, finely chopped
5 ml/1 tsp cornflour (cornstarch)
5 ml/1 tsp sesame oil
I small egg, beaten (size 4–5)

GARNISH

spring onion (scallion) curls (optional)
paprika

SERVES 2 OR 4

I clove garlic, chopped
2.5 cm/1 in piece fresh ginger, peeled and chopped
75 ml/5 tbsp soy sauce
¼ cup/60 ml/4 tbsp mirin (sweet rice wine) or dry sherry
¼ cup/60 ml/4 tbsp sake
30 ml/2 tbsp sugar
500 g/1 lb boned and skinned chicken meat, cut into 2.5 cm/1 in cubes
6–8 spring onions (scallions), trimmed and cut into 2.5 cm/1 in lengths
175 g/6 oz mushrooms, halved
½ cucumber, sliced, to garnish

YAKITORI CHICKEN SKEWERS

Mirin is available from Japanese food shops – but if you cannot obtain it, substitute with a dry sherry. Serve these skewers either as a starter, or with plain boiled rice as a main course. Chicken livers are sometimes included in Yakitori.

☐ In a bowl mix together the garlic, ginger, soy sauce, rice wine, sake and sugar. Stir in the chicken cubes. Cover with cling film and leave to marinate for 1 to 2 hours.

☐ Thread the chicken onto bamboo skewers 15–20 cm/6–8 in long, alternating with the spring onions and mushrooms. Brush with the marinade and arrange under a preheated grill.

☐ Cook for 8 to 10 minutes, basting frequently with the marinade, and turning the skewers several times, until the chicken is cooked through.

☐ Serve immediately, garnished with cucumber slices.

NOTE
Soak bamboo skewers for 30 minutes before using to prevent them from burning.

CHICKEN SATAY

This delicious Malaysian speciality can be made well in advance and chilled until required. Also try a combination of chicken, pork and beef. Serve the satays either as part of an oriental meal, or as a meal on its own, accompanied with plain boiled rice.

☐ Cut the chicken into 1.25 cm/½ in cubes.

☐ Combine the marinade ingredients in a bowl. Add the chicken cubes and stir until well coated. Cover and refrigerate for 2 hours, preferably overnight.

☐ Thread the meat onto 8 small bamboo skewers (see *Note*). Grill (broil) or barbecue for 6 to 8 minutes, turning frequently. (Use metal skewers if cooking over charcoal.)

☐ Meanwhile, make the sauce. Heat the oil in a pan, add the onon and garlic and cook until softened. Gradually blend in the spices, honey, soy sauce and lemon juice. Stir well, then add the peanut butter and cook gently for 1 minute.

☐ Remove from the heat and blend in the creamed coconut and hot water. Return to the heat and gradually bring to the boil stirring continuously. Reduce heat and simmer for 5 minutes. Taste and add salt if required.

☐ Arrange the skewered chicken on a platter, garnish with lemon twists and spring onion curls. Serve the peanut sauce separately in a bowl.

NOTE
Soak bamboo skewers for 30 minutes before using to prevent them from burning.

SERVES 4
500 g/1 lb chicken breasts or thighs, boned and skinned

MARINADE
1 small onion, peeled and grated
45 ml/3 tbsp soy sauce
45 ml/3 tbsp sherry
30 ml/2 tbsp vegetable oil
30 ml/2 tbsp clear honey
1 clove garlic, chopped
10 ml/2 tsp tomato purée (paste)
2.5 ml/½ tsp hot chilli (chili) powder

SATAY SAUCE
15 ml/1 tbsp vegetable oil
15 ml/1 tbsp grated onion
1 clove garlic, minced
2.5 ml/½ tsp hot chilli powder
2.5 ml/½ tsp ground coriander
10 ml/2 tsp honey
10 ml/2 tsp soy sauce
10 ml/2 tsp lemon juice
6 tbsp/75 g/3 oz smooth peanut butter
15 g/½ oz creamed coconut
1 ¼ cups/300 ml/½ pt water
salt

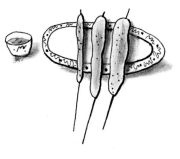

SESAME CHICKEN

While sesame seeds have a very subtle flavour and add a crunchiness here in contrast to the tender chicken strips, sesame oil is much stronger so the little used in this recipe is to add flavour rather than for frying purposes. Serve this dish hot with some stir-fried vegetables. It is also delicious cold, as a salad.

☐ Cut the chicken into fine diagonal shreds.

☐ Heat 15 ml/1 tbsp of the oil in a wok or frying pan (skillet) and stir-fry the chicken and dried chilli (chili) for 1 minute. Drain and transfer to absorbent kitchen paper.

☐ Wipe the wok clean, heat the remaining groundnut oil and add the sesame seeds. Stir-fry for 1 minute or until golden brown.

☐ Add the celery and stir-fry for a few seconds, before adding the remaining ingredients. Bring to the boil, return the chicken shreds and stir-fry for a further minute. Serve immediately.

SERVES 4
3 chicken breasts, boneless and skinned
(approx. 175 g/6 oz each)
30 ml/2 tbsp groundnut oil
5 ml/1 tsp dried chilli (chili) granules (or flakes)
15 ml/1 tbsp sesame seeds
2 sticks celery, trimmed and thiny sliced
15 ml/1 tbsp soy sauce
15 ml/1 tbsp dry sherry
5 ml/1 tsp cider vinegar
2.5 ml/½ tsp salt
5 ml/1 tsp sesame oil

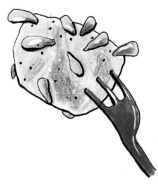

GINGERED CHICKEN WITH HONEY

SERVES 4

30 ml/2 tbsp sunflower oil
4 chicken breasts, skinned and part-boned (approx. 175 g/6 oz each)
5 cm/2 in root ginger, peeled and cut into tiny matchsticks
2 medium onions, peeled and sliced
10 ml/2 tsp ground ginger
¼ cup/60 ml/4 tbsp light soy sauce
¼ cup/60 ml/4 tbsp dry sherry
30 ml/2 tbsp clear honey
salt and freshly ground black pepper
3 spring onions (scallions), trimmed and finely chopped, to garnish

This dish is very simply prepared and best accompanied with pilau rice (see page 54).

☐ Heat the oil in a pan and sauté the chicken pieces until golden.
☐ Add the fresh ginger and onions to the oil and sauté until the onions soften. Stir in the ground ginger and cook for a further 2 minutes.
☐ Return the chicken to the pan and cook for a minute more, then pour on the soy sauce, dry sherry and honey.
☐ Cover with a tight-fitting lid and simmer for 30 minutes or until the chicken is tender.
☐ Transfer the chicken and onions to a warm serving dish. Turn up the heat and boil the sauce to reduce it slightly. Season to taste.
☐ Spoon the sauce over the chicken and garnish with a sprinkling of spring onions (scallions). Serve hot.

Gingered Chicken with Honey

CHICKEN WITH BLACK BEANS

SERVES 4

500 g/1 lb chicken pieces (thighs, wings, breasts)
15 ml/1 tbsp soy sauce
15 ml/1 tbsp dry sherry or rice wine
5 ml/1 tsp sugar
10 ml/2 tsp cornflour (cornstarch)
30 ml/2 tbsp groundnut oil
15 ml/1 tbsp finely chopped fresh ginger
4 cloves garlic, finely chopped
30 ml/2 tbsp black beans, rinsed and coarsely chopped
2 spring onions (scallions), finely chopped
½ sweet red (bell) pepper, cut into 2.5 cm/1 in squares
⅔ cup/150 ml/¼ pt chicken stock (broth)

Black soya beans are available from good Chinese supermarkets, and are sold either canned or packed in plastic bags (they need rinsing before use). These fermented, slightly salted beans partner the garlic and fresh ginger perfectly – to give a distinctive flavour, reminiscent of Chinese home cooking.

☐ Chop the chicken pieces into 5 cm/2 in chunks. Mix the soy sauce, dry sherry, sugar and cornflour (cornstarch). Stir into the chicken pieces and leave to marinate for 1 hour.
☐ Drain the chicken, discarding any marinade. Heat half the oil in a wok. Add the ginger and stir-fry briefly, then add the garlic and black beans. Cook for 2 to 3 minutes.
☐ Add the chicken pieces and stir-fry for 4 to 5 minutes until they are browned. Add the spring onion (scallion), red (bell) pepper and stock (broth), reduce heat and simmer for 10 minutes.
☐ Serve immediately with plain boiled rice.

TROPICAL STIR-FRY

The wonderful thing about stir-fry recipes is that any number or combination of ingredients can be used. Serve with plain boiled rice.

☐ Stir-fry the onion in half the oil for 3 minutes. Add the remaining oil, garlic and the chicken and stir-fry briskly until the chicken is evenly coloured and almost tender.

☐ Add the sunflower seeds and cashew nuts and stir-fry for a further minute. Add the mango, kiwi, kumquats and salt and pepper to taste. Stir fry for a further 2 to 3 minutes.

☐ Sprinkle with flaked coconut and serve immediately.

SERVES 4

I small onion, finely chopped
¼ cup/4 tbsp sunflower oil
I clove garlic, crushed (minced)
2 boneless chicken breasts (approx. 175 g/6 oz each), skinned and cut into thin strips
15 ml/1 tbsp sunflower seeds
40 g/1 ½ oz salted cashew nuts
½ ripe, pink skinned mango, stoned and thinly sliced
2 kiwi fruit, peeled and sliced
4 kumquats, halved
salt and freshly ground black pepper
30 ml/2 tbsp flaked coconut

Tropical Stir-Fry

Turmeric Chicken

TURMERIC CHICKEN

Very spicy, and full of Eastern promise – cardamom, dates, almonds and the characteristic yellow turmeric. Accompany with plain boiled rice and a refreshing cucumber or tomato salad to calm down the palate!

☐ Heat the oil in a pan, and sauté the chicken legs until golden brown. Remove to one side.

☐ Add the onion to the pan and sauté until golden brown. Reduce the heat and stir in the spices. Cook for 1 minute.

☐ Return the chicken legs to the pan. Sprinkle in the flour and gradually blend in the stock. Bring to the boil, then simmer for 30 minutes, or until the chicken is tender.

☐ Mix in the almonds, dates, yogurt and half the fresh coriander (cilantro). Simmer gently for a further 10 minutes.

☐ Serve hot, garnished with the remaining coriander (cilantro).

SERVES 6

¼ cup/60 ml/4 tbsp vegetable oil·
6 chicken leg portions (approx. 200 g/7 oz each)
2 medium onions, chopped
15 ml/1 tbsp ground coriander
5 ml/1 tsp turmeric
5 ml/1 tsp ground cumin
2.5 ml/½ tsp ground cardamom
2 pinches hot chilli (chili) powder
30 ml/2 tbsp plain (all purpose) flour
3 cups/750 ml/1 ¼ pt chicken stock (broth)
¼ cup/50 g/2 oz blanched almonds, coarsely chopped
¼ cup/50 g/2 oz dates, stoned and coarsely chopped
⅔ cup/150 ml/¼ pt natural low fat yogurt or fromage frais
30 ml/2 tbsp fresh coriander (cilantro) chopped
salt

175 g/6 oz mixed dried pulses (red kidney beans,
chick (garbanzos) peas, haricot (navy) beans etc)
1 clove garlic, finely chopped
1 medium onion, finely chopped
30 ml/2 tbsp vegetable oil
2.5 ml/½ tsp turmeric
2.5 ml/½ tsp ground cumin
8 medium chicken drumsticks
salt and freshly ground black pepper
6 tomatoes, seeded and chopped
2½ cups/600 ml/1 pt chicken stock (broth)
125 g/4 oz okra (ladies fingers)
freshly chopped parsley

SPICED BEAN CHICKEN

A feast full of protein with an Eastern flavour, serve with some naan bread and a crisp fresh salad.

- ☐ Soak the pulses in cold water overnight. Drain and put into a pan with enough fresh cold water to cover well, and boil steadily for 10 minutes. Drain thoroughly.
- ☐ Heat the oil in a large saucepan, add the onion and garlic and cook gently until softened.
- ☐ Add the spices and cook for a further minute then add the chicken drumsticks. Season to taste. Cook, stirring for 5 minutes until the chicken is coated with the spices.
- ☐ Add the tomatoes, stock, and drained pulses, cover and simmer gently for 45 to 60 minutes or until the beans are tender.
- ☐ Add the okra (ladies fingers) 5 minutes before the end of cooking.
- ☐ Serve piping hot sprinkled with fresh chopped parsley.

1 pkt or 2 pinches saffron strands
⅔ cup/150 ml/¼ pt hot water
30 ml/2 tbsp vegetable oil
1 × 1.75 kg/4 lb chicken, jointed
2 cloves garlic, finely chopped
5 ml/1 tsp ground cinnamon
5 ml/1 tsp ground ginger
1 large onion, finely chopped
75 g/3 oz dried apricots
¼ cup/60 ml/4 tbsp clear honey
salt and freshly ground black pepper
1 tbsp/15 g/½ oz butter
25 g/1 oz flaked almonds
2.5 ml/½ tsp paprika
fresh coriander (cilantro), to garnish

MOROCCAN CHICKEN WITH APRICOTS

This dish is reminiscent of 'Tagine' a stew cooked in the traditional Moroccan pointed earthenware pot. Honey was originally used to offset the saltiness of some meats and has remained one of the ingredients to this day.

- ☐ Soak the saffron strands in the hot water for 30 minutes.
- ☐ Heat the oil in a large pan, and sauté the chicken until well browned. Remove to one side.
- ☐ Sauté the garlic, cinnamon, ginger and onions until the onions are softened. Return the chicken to the pan. Season well.
- ☐ Add the apricots and pour on just enough boiling water to half cover the chicken joints. Cover and simmer for 30 minutes or until the chicken is just tender.
- ☐ Remove the chicken joints to a warm plate. Add the honey to the cooking juices and boil rapidly to reduce and thicken the sauce. Adjust seasoning.
- ☐ Return the chicken to the sauce and simmer for a further 10 minutes.
- ☐ Meanwhile melt the butter in a frying pan, add the flaked almonds and paprika and sauté until the almonds are golden brown.
- ☐ Serve the chicken accompanied with rice and sprinkled with the almonds. Garnish with sprigs of fresh coriander (cilantro).

CHICKEN TANDOORI STYLE

This dish can be prepared a day or two in advance and left, chilled, to marinate. It is equally good hot or cold, and served simply with a tomato and onion salad and freshly baked naan bread. The chicken can also be barbecued.

☐ Make several small incisions with the tip of a sharp knife in the chicken. Brush with the lemon juice.

☐ In a large bowl, blend together the yogurt, garlic, tomato purée (paste), ground spices and grated ginger. Add the chicken and mix well. Cover and leave to marinate for at least 6 hours, but preferably overnight.

☐ To make the yogurt dressing, mix all the ingredients thoroughly, season and chill until needed.

☐ Line an ovenproof dish with foil, place chicken and marinade in the dish, cover and bake for 45 minutes or until the chicken is tender. Remove foil and cook for a further 15 minutes or until browned. Accompany with the yogurt dressing.

SERVES 4 TO 6

6 boned chicken thighs, skinned
6 chicken drumsticks
30 ml/2 tbsp lemon juice
150 g/5 oz natural yogurt
2 cloves garlic, crushed
15 ml/1 tbsp tomato purée (paste)
5 ml/1 tsp ground cardamom
5 ml/1 tsp chilli (chili) powder
5 ml/1 tsp ground cumin
5 ml/1 tsp paprika
2.5 ml/½ tsp grated fresh ginger

YOGURT DRESSING
⅔ cup/150 ml/¼ pt natural yogurt
15 ml/1 tbsp chopped spring onions (scallions)
15 ml/1 tbsp chopped fresh mint
15 ml/1 tbsp chopped fresh coriander (cilantro)
salt and freshly ground black pepper

Oven temperature: 180 °C/350 °F/Gas 4

SERVES 4 TO 6

1 × 1.5 kg/3 lb chicken, oven-ready
30 ml/2 tbsp lemon juice
5 ml/1 tsp salt
25 g/1 oz ghee or 30 ml/2 tbsp vegetable oil
2 medium onions, sliced
4 cloves garlic, finely chopped
4 black cardamom pods, crushed
15 ml/1 tbsp poppy seeds
5 ml/1 tsp ground coriander (cilantro)
2.5 cm/1 in fresh ginger, peeled and finely chopped
5 ml/1 tsp chilli (chili) powder
2 pinches ground cloves
1 ¼ cups/300 ml/½ pt natural yogurt
60 ml/4 tbsp freshly chopped coriander (cilantro)

GARNISH
1 small cucumber, thinly sliced
sprigs fresh coriander (cilantro)

Oven temperature: 200 °C/400 °F/Gas 6

MURGH MASSALLAM

Although there are now many variations of this dish, it originated from a north Indian curry, and is always served as a whole chicken with a yogurt sauce. Some recipes also suggest a stuffing of sultanas (golden raisins), hard boiled (hard cooked) egg and onions. Serve the chicken with a vegetable dish and Indian bread, such as chapati.

☐ Prick the chicken all over, and rub in the lemon juice and salt. Place in a roasting tray, cover with cling film and leave to stand for 30 minutes.

☐ Heat the ghee or vegetable oil in a pan. Sauté the onions and garlic until crisp and golden.

☐ Stir in the caradamom pods, poppy seeds, ground coriander, fresh ginger, chilli (chili) powder and ground cloves and cook for a further minute.

☐ Remove from the heat. Blend in the yogurt and freshly chopped coriander (cilantro). Rub the mixture all over the chicken. If possible, leave to stand for 2 to 3 hours (cover and chill in refrigerator).

☐ Cook the chicken for 1 to 1 ¼ hours or until tender. Transfer the chicken to a heated serving platter and keep warm.

☐ Skim off any fat from the juices in the roasting pan. Place the tin over a medium heat and bring to the boil, stirring well. It will thicken slightly.

☐ Pour the sauce over the chicken and surround with slices of cucumber and garnish with sprigs of fresh coriander (cilantro).

SERVES 4

750 g/1 ½ lb boneless chicken, cubed
MARINADE
1 small onion, finely chopped
2 cloves garlic, finely chopped
2.5 ml/½ tsp salt
5 ml/1 tsp hot chilli (chili) powder
5 ml/1 tsp paprika
2.5 ml/½ tsp ground ginger
(or 5 ml/1 tsp grated fresh ginger)
2.5 ml/½ tsp ground cumin
15 ml/1 tbsp lemon juice
⅔ cup/150 ml/¼ pt natural yogurt

MINT CHUTNEY
45 ml/3 tbsp mint sauce
10 ml/2 tsp chilli (chili) powder
1 small onion, finely chopped
5 ml/1 tsp salt

GARNISH
onion rings
lemon wedges

CHICKEN TIKKA WITH MINT CHUTNEY

These chicken tikka kebabs can be barbecued or grilled, and are accompanied with a mint relish. Serve the kebabs as a starter to an Indian meal or as a main course. They are very good cold, in a lunch box or picnic.

☐ Grind the onions and garlic to a paste with the salt. Blend in the spices and lemon juice and mix into the yogurt.

☐ Stir in the chicken, cover and leave to marinate for 1 to 2 hours.

☐ Thread the chicken onto skewers and cook under a hot grill for 10 to 15 minutes or until the chicken is tender.

☐ Meanwhile, make the Mint Chutney by mixing together all the ingredients. Chill.

☐ Garnish the tikka kebabs with onion rings and lemon wedges, and serve with the Mint Chutney and chapatis or naan bread.

CHICKEN KASHMIR

For those who like a milder, more subtle Indian dish, this is ideal. The selected spices are 'warm' rather than 'hot' and the sauce is creamy.

☐ Cut the chicken into bite-size pieces. Place in a bowl with the yogurt, coriander, cumin, cinnamon, coriander seeds, ground ginger and a little salt and stir until well coated. Cover and chill for 4 hours, but preferably overnight.

☐ Heat the oil in a pan, add the onion and garlic and sauté until softened and golden. Strain the chicken pieces and add to the pan. Sauté until sealed.

☐ Sprinkle on the flour, then blend in the chicken stock (broth). Add the creamed coconut and stir until it dissolves and the mixture thickens.

☐ Pour in the remaining yogurt and spice marinade. Cover and simmer for 25 minutes or until the chicken is tender. Adjust seasoning, if necessary.

☐ Five minutes before the end, stir in the chopped coriander (cilantro).

☐ Serve the chicken, sprinkled with the toasted almonds and accompanied with rice.

CREAMY COCONUT CHICKEN CURRY

The subtle coconut flavour is obtained by infusing dessicated (shredded) coconut in milk or water. This needs to be prepared in advance, but will result in an authentic addition to curries. Serve this creamy curry with plain boiled rice and a banana or tomato salad.

☐ Pour the boiling water and milk over the dessicated (shredded) coconut in a bowl. Stir and leave to infuse for about 2 hours. Strain the liquid, squeezing well, and discard the coconut.

☐ Heat the oil in a pan, add the chicken pieces a few at a time, and cook until golden brown, for 6 to 8 minutes. Remove to one side.

☐ Add the onions and garlic and ginger to the pan and cook for 1 minute. Sprinkle on the curry powder and flour and cook, stirring to a paste, for a further minute.

☐ Gradually blend in the stock and coconut milk and slowly bring to the boil, stirring, until thickened.

☐ Return the chicken to the pan together with the sultanas (golden raisins) and flaked coconut. Cover and simmer for 25 minutes.

☐ Remove lid and simmer for a further 15 minutes or until the sauce has reduced and thickened slightly more. Add the lemon juice and salt, to taste.

☐ Remove the pan from the heat, swirl in the yogurt and serve immediately.

SERVES 4

750 g/1 ½ lb boneless chicken, cubed (breast or thigh)
⅔ cup/150 ml/¼ pt natural yogurt
5 ml/1 tsp ground coriander
5 ml/1 tsp ground cumin
5 ml/1 tsp ground cinnamon
2.5 ml/½ tsp coriander (cilantro) seeds
2.5 ml/½ tsp ground ginger
salt
15 ml/1 tbsp vegetable oil
1 medium onion, sliced
1 clove garlic, finely chopped
15 ml/1 tbsp plain (all purpose) flour
⅓ cup/90 ml/6 tbsp chicken stock (broth)
25 g/1 oz creamed coconut
45 ml/3 tbsp freshly chopped coriander (cilantro)
25 g/1 oz flaked almonds, toasted, to garnish

Chicken Kashmir

SERVES 4

⅔ cup/150 ml/¼ pt boiling water
⅔ cup/150 ml/¼ pt milk
½ cup/125 g/4 oz dessicated (shredded) coconut
30 ml/2 tbsp groundnut oil
1 x 1.5 kg/3 lb chicken, jointed and skinned
2 onions, finely chopped
1 clove garlic, finely chopped
10 ml/2 tsp grated fresh ginger
30 ml/2 tbsp mild curry powder
15 g/½ oz plain (all purpose) flour
1 ¼ cups/300 ml/½ pt chicken stock (broth)
¼ cup/50 g/2 oz sultanas (golden raisins)
¼ cup/50 g/2 oz flaked coconut
5 ml/1 tsp salt
15 ml/1 tbsp lemon juice
⅓ cup/90 ml/6 tbsp natural yogurt

SERVES 4

30 ml/2 tbsp vegetable oil
250 g/8 oz onions, sliced
30 ml/2 tbsp hot curry powder
25 g/1 oz plain (all purpose) flour
1 large can mangoes in light syrup
(approximately 400 g/13 oz)
chicken stock (broth)
½ cup/125 g/4 oz raisins
15 g/½ oz dessicated (shredded) coconut
2.5 ml/½ teaspoon salt
500 g/1 lb cooked chicken, cut into bite-size pieces

Chicken Curry with Mangoes

SERVES 4

30 ml/2 tbsp ground coriander (cilantro)
15 ml/1 tbsp ground cumin
10 ml/2 tsp turmeric
5 ml/1 tsp ground cinnamon
5 ml/1 tsp chilli (chili) powder
2.5 ml/½ tsp grated nutmeg
8 small chicken joints (wings, thighs, drumsticks)
skinned
60 ml/4 tbsp vegetable oil
250 g/8 oz onions, finely chopped
25 g/1 oz fresh ginger, peeled and chopped
2 cloves garlic, peeled and chopped
2 cardamom pods (seeds only)
4 cloves
5 ml/1 tsp dried chillies (chilis)
2½ cups/600 ml/1 pt hot chicken stock (broth)
500 g/1 lb potatoes, peeled and cut into chunks
500 g/1 lb carrots, peeled and cut into chunks
1 cup/250 ml/8 fl oz hot milk
1 cup/125 g/4 oz dessicated (shredded) coconut
30 ml/2 tbsp cornflour (cornstarch)
15 ml/1 tbsp lemon juice
15 ml/1 tbsp black treacle
fresh chopped coriander (cilantro) to garnish

CHICKEN CURRY WITH MANGOES

This is a quick, convenient way of using up cooked chicken meat by making it stretch into another delicious meal. Canned mangoes are used, again as a convenience, but can be substituted with what suits your store cupboard – pineapple and peaches are just as good.

- ☐ Heat the oil in a large saucepan. Add the onions and sauté until softened and just turning golden.
- ☐ Stir in the curry powder and flour and cook for a further minute.
- ☐ Drain the mangoes. Measure the juice and make up to 3 cups/750 ml/1¼pt with the chicken stock. Cut the fruit into bite-size pieces.
- ☐ Blend the stock into the onion mixture, and bring to the boil, stirring. Add the raisins, coconut and salt.
- ☐ Stir in the chicken meat, cover and simmer for 30 minutes. Five minutes before the end, add the pieces of mango.
- ☐ Serve accompanied with plain boiled rice and poppadums.

NOTE
Do not reheat this dish.

MALAYSIAN CHICKEN CURRY

This curry is a complete meal on its own – I've chosen to include carrots and potatoes, but cauliflower and green (string or snap) beans would also be good. Accompany with poppadums and a fresh tomato salad to cool the palate!

- ☐ Mix the first six ingredients together in a bowl, and add the dry chicken joints. Mix well, rubbing the spices into the surface of the chicken.
- ☐ Heat the oil in a large heavy-based pan, and fry the onions, ginger and garlic until softened and golden. Add the cardamom seeds, cloves, chillies (chilis) and any loose powder from the chicken spice mix. Cook for a further minute, scraping the bottom of the pan well.
- ☐ Add the chicken and cook, turning occasionally, for 3 to 4 minutes or until the surface of the chicken seals. Pour over the hot stock (broth), and a little salt, to taste. Cover and simmer for 15 to 20 minutes.
- ☐ Stir in the potato and carrot chunks, cover and simmer for a further 40 minutes.
- ☐ Meanwhile, pour the hot milk over the dessicated (shredded) coconut and leave to infuse for ½ hour. Squeeze the liquid through a fine sieve or muslin. Blend with the cornflour and lemon juice and stir into the curry. Simmer, uncovered, until thickened.
- ☐ Stir in the treacle. Correct seasoning and serve, garnished with freshly chopped coriander (cilantro).

EVERYDAY MAIN MEALS

STUFFED POUSSIN (CORNISH GAME HEN) WITH MUSHROOM SAUCE

Although very tender and succulent, baby poussins (Cornish game hens) do not have as pronounced a flavour as the maturer chicken. They are delicious stuffed and served with a sauce – and there is no need to worry about carving or jointing the bird!

- ☐ Sauté the bacon strips in a dry pan until the fat begins to run. Add the onions, celery, herbs and lemon juice and rind. Cook until the onions have softened.
- ☐ Meanwhile, in a liquidizer or processor, work the bread down to crumbs. Place in a bowl together with the walnuts and raisins.
- ☐ Mix the bacon mixture into the crumbs together with the beaten eggs. Season to taste. Divide between the birds, packing the stuffing well into the neck cavity.
- ☐ Transfer the poussins (Cornish game hens) into a shallow roasting tin (pan). Brush with the oil and cook for 45 to 50 minutes. Transfer to a warm serving plate. Retain the juices.
- ☐ Pour the juices into a saucepan, or alternatively transfer the roasting tin onto the hotplate. Stir in the sherry, and 'deglaze' the tin (pan), if using, scraping loose any residue.
- ☐ Add the mushrooms and all but 15 ml/1 tbsp of the stock (broth) and bring to the boil.
- ☐ Blend the cornflour (cornstarch) with the reserved stock (broth) and stir it into the sauce. Stir until the sauce has thickened.
- ☐ Reduce the heat to a simmer and stir in the single (cereal) cream and mustard. Adjust seasonings.
- ☐ Garnish each poussin (Cornish game hen) with a small bunch of fresh watercress and spoon some sauce around the bird. Serve immediately.

SERVES 4

375 g/12 oz streaky bacon, cut into strips
2 large onions, finely chopped
1 stick celery, finely chopped
15 ml/1 tbsp mixed fresh herbs, chopped
rind and juice ½ lemon
1 small brown loaf (2-day old), crusts removed
¼ cup/50 g/2 oz walnuts, coarsely chopped
¼ cup/50 g/2 oz raisins
2 eggs, beaten
4 poussins (Cornish game hens)
(approx. 500 g/1 lb each)

SAUCE

¼ cup/60 ml/4 tbsp dry sherry
1 cup/125 g/4 oz button mushrooms, sliced
½ cup/125 ml/4 fl oz chicken stock (broth)
5 ml/1 tsp cornflour (cornstarch)
½ cup/125 ml/4 fl oz single (light) cream
5 ml/1 tsp Dijon mustard

GARNISH

fresh watercress

Oven temperature: 210 °C/425 °F/Gas 7

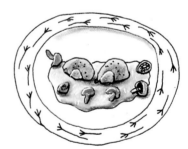

SERVES 4

1 × 1.5 kg/3 ½ lb oven-ready chicken
30 ml/2 tbsp vegetable oil
2 medium onions, peeled and thinly sliced
10 ml/2 tsp paprika
½ cup/125 ml/4 fl oz dry white wine
500 g/1 lb tomatoes, deseeded and chopped
(or 1 × 425 g/14 oz can tomatoes)
15 ml/1 tbsp tomato purée (paste)
2 whole canned pimentos (sweet red pepper),
roughly chopped
bouquet garni
salt
¼ cup/60 ml/4 tbsp natural yogurt
15 ml/1 tbsp chopped parsley

PAPRIKA CHICKEN

Paprika chicken uses, as the name implies, the subtle, milder dried red pepper – never to be confused or substituted for hotter members of the family like Cayenne or chilli (chili). Serve this warming dish with noodles or pasta shells.

☐ Joint the chicken into 8 pieces (*see page 10*), and remove the skin where possible.

☐ Heat the oil in a large pan and sauté the chicken until browned. Remove and set aside. Add the onions to the pan and cook until softened.

☐ Sprinkle in the paprika and cook for a further minute. Blend in the wine.

☐ Return the chicken pieces to the pan together with the tomatoes, purée (paste), pimentos (sweet red peppers), bouquet garni and salt to taste. Cover and simmer for 45 minutes.

☐ Transfer the chicken to a serving dish to keep warm. Rub the contents of the pan through a sieve. Return to rinsed pan and reheat. Season to taste.

☐ Swirl in the yogurt and pour over the chicken pieces. Sprinkle with the chopped parsley. Serve immediately.

PARMESAN BAKED CHICKEN

A topping rich with tomatoes, herbs and Italian cheeses embraces succulent breasts of chicken. Serve with plain new potatoes and fresh spinach.

- ☐ Heat half the oil in a pan and sauté the onions, garlic and celery until softened. Stir in the tomatoes, purée (paste), Tobasco, herbs and sugar. Season with salt and pepper. Simmer, uncovered, for 25 to 30 minutes.
- ☐ Sprinkle the skinned chicken breasts with lemon juice. Dip each breast into the egg and then the seasoned flour. Shake off any excess.
- ☐ Heat the remaining oil in a non-stick frying pan and sauté the chicken breasts for 5 minutes, turning halfway through, until golden brown. Drain on absorbent kitchen paper.
- ☐ Lay the chicken in an ovenproof dish and cover with half the Mozzarella cheese. Pour over sauce, top with the remaining cheese, and sprinkle with Parmesan.
- ☐ Bake for 25 to 30 minutes or until bubbling and golden.
- ☐ Serve, garnished with fresh watercress.

SERVES 4

4 boneless chicken breasts (approx. 150 g/5 oz each)
30 ml/2 tbsp olive oil
2 medium onions, finely chopped
2 cloves garlic, finely chopped
1 stick celery, chopped
1 × 425 g/14 oz can chopped tomatoes
15 ml/1 tbsp tomato purée (paste)
few drops Tobasco
5 ml/1 tsp fresh basil, chopped
5 ml/1 tsp fresh marjoram, chopped
5 ml/1 tsp sugar
30 ml/2 tbsp lemon juice
1 egg, beaten
25 g/1 oz plain (all purpose) flour, seasoned
150 g/6 oz Mozzarella cheese, grated
30 ml/2 tbsp grated Parmesan cheese
salt and freshly ground black pepper
fresh watercress, to garnish

Oven temperature: 180 °C/350 °F/Gas 5

Chicken Thighs in Pernod

Parmesan Baked Chicken

CHICKEN THIGHS IN PERNOD

A quick and easy standby, good enough on its own with crusty brown bread, or served with fresh vegetables.

- ☐ Heat the oil in a large pan. Cook the chicken for 8 minutes, browning all sides. Reduce the heat, add the shallots or onion and water. Cover the pan and simmer gently for 30 to 35 minutes or until the chicken is tender.
- ☐ Remove the lid, increase the heat and pour in the Pernod. Set alight with a match, and turn off the heat. When the flames die down, scrape up any sediment from the bottom of the pan.
- ☐ Remove the chicken portions to a warm serving dish. Season the remaining juices with salt and pepper and bring to the boil. Spoon over the chicken and serve, garnished with a sprinkling of parsley.

SERVES 4

8–12 chicken thighs (depending on size)
30 ml/2 tbsp vegetable oil
2 shallots or 1 small sweet onion, finely chopped
¼ cup/60 ml/4 tbsp water
⅓ cup/90 ml/6 tbsp Pernod
salt and freshly ground black pepper
chopped fresh parsley, to garnish

SERVES 4

4 chicken joints, skinned (approx. 200 g/7 oz each)
25 g/1 oz plain (all purpose) flour, seasoned
45 ml/3 tbsp vegetable oil
8 pickling onions or shallots, peeled
1 clove garlic, finely chopped
1 cup/125 g/4 oz button mushrooms, halved
1 sweet green (bell) pepper, deseeded and cut into strips
2 cups/450 ml/¾ pt chopped tomatoes and juice (canned)
⅔ cup/150 ml/¼ pt dry white wine
30 ml/2 tbsp tomato purée (paste)
30 ml/2 tbsp red wine vinegar
5 ml/1 tsp chopped fresh basil
5 ml/1 tsp chopped fresh oregano
salt and freshly ground black pepper, to taste
50 g/2 oz black olives
chopped basil or parsley, to garnish

Chicken Cacciatore

CHICKEN CACCIATORE

This Italian dish is delicious simply served on a bed of spaghetti.

☐ Skin the chicken joints and dust them with the seasoned flour. Heat the oil in a large pan and sauté the chicken until golden brown.

☐ Add the onions and garlic and cook for a further 4 minutes. Sprinkle in any remaining flour, the mushrooms and green (bell) pepper and gradually blend in the tomatoes and juice. Stir in the remaining ingredients apart from the olives. Check seasoning.

☐ Cover and simmer for 20 to 30 minutes or until chicken is tender. Ten minutes before the end, stir in the olives.

☐ Serve, garnished with freshly chopped basil or parsley.

SERVES 2 TO 3

250 g/8 oz chicken livers, halved
¼ cup/25 g/1 oz plain (all purpose) flour
salt and freshly ground black pepper
30 ml/2 tbsp olive oil
125 g/4 oz cooked ham, cut into julienne strips (see Glossary, page 93)
⅓ cup/90 ml/6 tbsp port
¾ cup/175 ml/6 fl oz chicken stock (broth)
30 ml/2 tbsp chopped parsley

GARNISH

1 small cucumber, cut into thick slices, seeds removed
2 tbsp/25 g/1 oz butter

SAUTÉED CHICKEN LIVERS

Chicken livers are generally sold frozen and are economical, nutritious and require little preparation. Always cut away any green tinged liver, which will taste bitter, and wash and dry them well. This recipe is very quick to prepare and good accompanied with creamed potato or noodles.

☐ Dust the chicken livers with the flour seasoned with salt and pepper.

☐ Heat the oil in a frying pan and sauté the ham for 1 minute.

☐ Add the livers and sauté for 2 minutes.

☐ Pour in the port and stock (broth). Cook gently for 5 minutes, stirring frequently.

☐ Meanwhile prepare the garnish. Parboil the cucumber for 2 to 3 minutes, drain and dry. Melt the butter and sauté the cucumber until transluscent.

☐ Stir the parsley into the chicken livers and serve with the cucumber rings.

CHICKEN IN SHARP SAUCE

A lively, piquant flavour transforms these economical chicken thighs into a special treat. Accompany with some plain boiled new potatoes and sweet early season peas.

- ☐ Heat the oil in a large heavy-based saucepan. Cook the chicken thighs, turning, until evenly browned. Add the garlic cloves, and reduce the heat. Cover and simmer for 20 minutes or until the chicken is tender
- ☐ Drain all but 15 ml/1 tbsp fat from the pan. Add the vinegar and stir well, scraping up any sediment from the bottom. Boil rapidly until the liquid is reduced to approximately 30 ml/2 tbsp. Transfer the chicken to a serving dish and keep warm.
- ☐ Add the wine, brandy, mustard and tomato purée (paste) to the pan, stir well and rapidly boil until reduced to a thick sauce (approximately 5 minutes).
- ☐ In another small saucepan, heat the fromage frais until warmed through. Place a sieve over the saucepan, and pour on the vinegar sauce, pressing the garlic cloves well to remove the pulp. Remove sieve. Season, to taste.
- ☐ Stir the tomatoes into the sauce. Reheat if necessary and pour over the chicken to serve.

SERVES 4

8 chicken thighs
30 ml/2 tbsp sunflower oil
5 whole cloves garlic, unpeeled
75 ml/5 tbsp red wine vinegar
1 1/4/300 ml/1/2 pt dry white wine
30 ml/2 tbsp brandy
10 ml/2 tsp Dijon mustard
10 ml/2 tsp tomato purée (paste)
2/3 cup/150 ml/1/4 pt low fat fromage frais
2 tomatoes, skinned and deseeded and cut into thin strips
salt and freshly ground black pepper

Chicken in Sharp Sauce

Greek Style Chicken

GREEK STYLE CHICKEN

Serve this fragrant dish piping hot with a crisp salad and a bowl of Greek yogurt dressing,such as tzatsiki.

- ☐ Cut the chicken leg portions in half with a meat cleaver or very sharp knife. (Follow the fine white line on the underside of the leg.)
- ☐ Place the chicken into a large shallow ovenproof dish with the onions, garlic, lemon, potatoes, thyme, half the olive oil and a little salt and pepper.
- ☐ Drizzle over the remaining olive oil, cover with foil, and cook for 30 minutes, stirring once or twice, until the chicken is tender and the potatoes and onions are a good colour.
- ☐ Serve hot, garnished, if you like, with a sprinkling of freshly chopped thyme.

SERVES 4

4 chicken leg portions
2 medium red-skinned onions, peeled and quartered
4 cloves garlic, chopped
2 lemons, cut into chunks
375 g/12 oz new potatoes, scrubbed and halved
15 ml/1 tbsp chopped fresh thyme
(or 5 ml/1 tsp dried thyme)
1/4 cup/60 ml/4 tbsp olive oil
salt and freshly ground black pepper
freshly chopped thyme, to garnish (optional)

Oven temperature: 190 °C/375 °F/Gas Mark 5

SERVES 4

500 g/1 lb chicken livers
1 tbsp/15 g/½ oz butter
15 ml/1 tbsp vegetable oil
1 large onion, diced
1 clove garlic, crushed
2.5 ml/½ tsp hot chilli (chili) powder
3 tomatoes, peeled, deseeded and sliced
⅔ cup/75 g/3 oz button mushrooms, sliced
30 ml/2 tbsp tomato purée (paste)
½ cup/125 ml/4 fl oz red wine or Marsala
2.5 ml/½ tsp thyme, freshly chopped
pinch ground bayleaves
5 ml/1 tsp Worcestershire sauce
salt and freshly ground black pepper
⅔ cup/150 ml/¼ pt fromage frais
freshly chopped parsley, to garnish

BLUSHING CHICKEN LIVERS

Here the chicken livers are quickly cooked in a spicy tomato sauce. They are good served with jacket potatoes, creamed potatoes or noodles and a green salad.

□ Rinse the chicken livers and pat dry on kitchen paper towel.
□ Heat the butter and oil in a saucepan. Sauté the onions and garlic until lightly browned and softened.
□ Sprinkle in the chilli (chili) powder and stir in the chicken livers. Cook for 4 minutes.
□ Add the tomatoes and mushrooms and cook for a further minute. Then stir in the tomato purée (paste), red wine or Marsala, herbs and Worcestershire sauce. Simmer, uncovered, for 4 minutes. The liquid will reduce a little.
□ Season to taste and stir in the fromage frais.
□ Serve immediately, garnished liberally with chopped parsley.

FRAGRANT CHICKEN PARCELS

These parcels, containing fresh herbs, yogurt and succulent chicken, can be cooked in the oven, over a steamer or even in with the barbecue charcoals. Whichever method is chosen, the result is deliciously aromatic. Accompany with new potatoes and green (string or snap) beans.

☐ In a shallow dish, blend together the first nine ingredients. Make a couple of slashes in the chicken breasts, then coat the chicken with the sauce. Leave in the dish, cover and marinate for 2 to 3 hours in a cool place.

☐ Place each breast in the centre of a large piece of foil. Spoon over any remaining marinade. Wrap the foil up around the chicken, sealing well.

☐ Cook for 20 to 25 minutes or until the chicken is tender. Serve in the foil parcels, opened and garnished with lemon slices and fresh chervil.

NOTE

If you would prefer to steam the chicken parcels they will take 25 to 30 minutes.

SERVES 4

5 ml/1 tsp cornflour (cornstarch)
grated rind ½ lemon
45 ml/3 tbsp natural yogurt
3 cardamom pods, seeds only, crushed
2.5 ml/½ tsp coriander seeds, crushed¹ (cilantro)
15 ml/1 tbsp freshly chopped chervil
10 ml/2 tsp freshly chopped tarragon
10 ml/2 tsp Dijon mustard
salt and freshly ground black pepper
4 boneless chicken breasts (approx. 175 g/6 oz) skinned

GARNISH
lemon slices
fresh chervil

Oven temperature: 190 °C/375 °C/Gas 6

Fragrant Chicken Parcels

Chicken Jurassiene

CHICKEN JURASSIENNE

Although this recipe uses whole chicken breasts, you can, if you prefer, cut the chicken into 'goujons' (wide strips) before crumbing them. Serve accompanied with mixed salad.

☐ Slightly flatten the chicken breasts between 2 sheets of dampened greaseproof paper.

☐ Mix together the flour, nutmeg and salt and pepper and thoroughly coat the chicken breasts.

☐ Dip the floured chicken breasts in the beaten egg, then into a mixture of breadcrumbs and cheese, pressing the crumbs well against the chicken flesh.

☐ Place on a lightly oiled baking tray (cookie sheet). Drizzle the oil over the breasts. Cook for 30 minutes or until golden brown and crisp.

☐ Serve hot, garnished with lemon slices.

SERVES 4

4 chicken boneless breasts (approx. 150 g/5 oz each) skinned
½ cup/50 g/2 oz plain (all purpose) flour
2 pinches grated nutmeg
salt and freshly ground black pepper
2 eggs, lightly beaten
1½ cups/75 g/3 oz fresh breadcrumbs
40 g/1½ oz Gruyère cheese, finely grated
¼ cup/60 ml/4 tbsp sunflower oil
1 lemon, sliced, to garnish

Oven temperature: 200 °C/400 °F/Gas 6

FRUITY CHICKEN KEBABS WITH CURRIED HONEY GLAZE

Kebabs are perfect for both a summer barbecue or a winter supper. They can be made well in advance and the ingredients can be varied to suit your own preference. Fruit and a curried honey marinade are delicious with chicken and help to keep it moist during cooking.

- ☐ Shake all the marinade ingredients together in a screw top jar.
- ☐ Cut the chicken into neat 2.5 cm/1 in cubes. Place in a bowl and pour over the marinade. Cover and keep in a refrigerator for 6 hours, or until required.
- ☐ Stretch the bacon rashers with the back of a knife. Cut each into half and form into rolls.
- ☐ Alternately thread pieces of chicken, apricot halves, banana chunks and bacon rolls onto skewers.
- ☐ Brush with the remaining marinade and cook for 10 to 15 minutes under a pre-heated grill (broiler) turning and basting frequently, until the chicken is cooked and sizzling.
- ☐ Serve warm with crusty bread and salad.

NOTE

If you are using bamboo skewers, soak these in water for 30 minutes beforehand to prevent them from burning.

SERVES 4

MARINADE
1/3 cup/90 ml/6 tbsp clear honey
1/4 cup/60 ml/4 tbsp light olive oil
rind and juice 1 orange
2 cloves garlic, crushed
15 ml/1 tbsp Worcestershire sauce
5 ml/1 tsp coriander seeds, crushed
5 ml/1 tsp curry powder
salt

4 large boneless chicken breasts, skinned
8 rashers streaky bacon, diced
16 dried apricot halves (non-soak variety)
2 firm bananas, cut into 2.5 cm/1 in slices
15 ml/1 tbsp lemon juice

BARBECUED ROAST CHICKEN

This recipe makes a change from the traditional roast. The chicken is coated with a barbecue sauce and roasted in the delicious juices. Alternatively, the sauce can be poured over an equivalent quantity of chicken drumsticks and thighs and cooked for 1 hour instead. Serve with jacket potatoes or boiled rice and seasonal or stir-fried vegetables.

- ☐ Place the chicken in a roasting tin (pan). Rub the oil over the chicken and season with salt and pepper.
- ☐ Roast the chicken for 30 minutes.
- ☐ In a screw-top jar or bowl, mix together the remaining ingredients, apart from the garnish. Remove the chicken from the oven and pour the sauce over the bird.
- ☐ Roast for a further 1 hour, basting frequently with the sauce. The skin will turn a rich, dark-brown colour.
- ☐ Serve the chicken hot, garnished with fresh sprigs of watercress.

SERVES 4

1 × 1.5 kg/3½ lb oven-ready chicken
15 ml/1 tbsp olive oil
salt and freshly ground black pepper
1 medium onion, finely diced
1/4 cup/60 ml/4 tbsp cider or sherry vinegar
1/4 cup/2 tbsp tomato purée (paste)
15 ml/1 tbsp clear honey
5 ml/1 tsp mustard powder
1 clove garlic, crushed
fresh watercress, to garnish

Oven temperature: 200 °C/400 °F/Gas 6

Fruity Chicken Kebabs with Curried Honey Glaze

SERVES 4

1 × 1.5 kg/3½ lb oven-ready chicken, jointed
(see page 10)
juice of ½ lemon
30 ml/2 tbsp sunflower oil
1 onion, quartered
1 stick celery, chopped
1 carrot, peeled and chopped
1 sprig fresh tarragon
6 black peppercorns
salt

SAUCE

15 ml/1 tbsp butter
15 ml/1 tbsp sunflower oil
1 clove garlic, finely chopped
30 ml/2 tbsp fresh tarragon, chopped
5 ml/1 tsp Dijon mustard
½ cup/125 g/4 fl oz chicken stock (broth)
½ cup/125 ml/4 fl oz fromage frais
15 ml/1 tbsp brandy (optional)
salt and freshly ground black pepper

GARNISH

lemon slices
fresh tarragon sprigs

TARRAGON CHICKEN

Tarragon is a classic herb to accompany chicken. It has a powerful flavour and a tendency to turn bitter if cooked for too long, so care is required when using it.

- ☐ Skin the chicken pieces and rub with the lemon juice.
- ☐ Heat the oil in a pan and sauté the chicken pieces until well browned.
- ☐ Add the remaining ingredients and pour on just enough cold water to half cover the chicken.
- ☐ Cover with a tight fitting lid. Bring to the boil, then reduce to a simmer for 45 minutes or until the chicken is tender.
- ☐ Remove chicken and keep warm while making the sauce.
- ☐ Strain the cooking liquor into a measuring jug.
- ☐ Heat the butter and the sunflower oil and sauté the garlic until softened. Stir in the tarragon and mustard and cook for a further minute.
- ☐ Pour on the chicken stock and brandy, if used. Adjust seasoning to taste. Bring to the boil for 1 minute then reduce heat. Stir in the fromage frais.
- ☐ Spoon the sauce over the served chicken pieces and garnish with a twist of lemon and fresh sprigs of tarragon.

BAKED CHICKEN WITH BASIL SAUCE

Fresh basil is vital for this flavoursome dish and really has no substitute. Accompany with fresh green (string or snap) beans.

- ☐ Place the chicken joints in a shallow baking dish.
- ☐ In a bowl, mix together the breadcrumbs, bacon, cheese, parsley, garlic and mustard powder. Sprinkle on the Worcestershire sauce and season to taste.
- ☐ Press the crumb mixture on top of each chicken joint. Dot with small pieces of butter and drizzle on the oil.
- ☐ Cook for 35 to 40 minutes or until the chicken is tender. (Cover the joints with foil if they get too brown.)
- ☐ Meanwhile, make the Basil Sauce. Combine the oil, vinegar, garlic and basil leaves in a saucepan. Bring to the boil, then immediately reduce heat to a simmer.
- ☐ Stir in the fromage frais and the cornflour (cornstarch), blended with the water. Stir until heated through and thickened. Season to taste.
- ☐ Transfer the baked chicken to a warm serving plate and pour the sauce over the centre of the joints. Garnish with fresh basil leaves.

SERVES 4

4 chicken joints, skinned
1 cup/50 g/2 oz fresh white breadcrumbs
50 g/2 oz bacon, derinded, and chopped
25 g/1 oz Parmesan cheese, freshly grated
15 ml/1 tbsp parsley, chopped
2 cloves garlic, finely chopped
2.5 ml/½ tsp mustard powder
10 ml/2 tsp Worcestershire sauce
salt and freshly ground black pepper
25 g/1 oz butter
15 ml/1 tbsp olive oil

BASIL SAUCE
¼ cup/60 ml/4 tbsp olive oil
¼ cup/60 ml/4 tbsp white wine vinegar
1 clove garlic, finely chopped
1 cup/50 g/2 oz fresh basil leaves, finely chopped
½ cup/125 ml/4 fl oz fromage frais or natural yogurt
5 ml/1 tsp cornflour (cornstarch)
5 ml/1 tsp water
salt and freshly ground black pepper

GARNISH
fresh basil leaves

Oven temperature: 190 °C/375 °F/Gas 5

POACHED CHICKEN WITH ALMOND AND HORSERADISH SAUCE

The addition of horseradish adds a pungent flavour to this chicken dish; yet it may have your guests trying to identify the 'mystery ingredient'.

- ☐ Place the chicken in a large pan. Add the carrot, onion, bayleaf, peppercorns and cloves. Pour on enough cold water to cover the chicken. Gradually bring to the boil, then reduce heat and simmer, covered, for 2 to 2½ hours or until tender.
- ☐ Remove the chicken, skin and joint it and keep warm in a covered serving dish. Strain off and reserve 2½ cups/600 ml/1 pt of the stock (broth) for the sauce.
- ☐ Melt the butter in a pan and blend in the flour. Cook for a minute. Remove from the heat and gradually blend in the stock (broth). Return to the heat and stir, until thickened.
- ☐ Stir in the horseradish relish, chopped almonds and parsley. Simmer for 5 minutes. Add the fromage frais and warm through. Season.
- ☐ Spoon the sauce over the chicken and garnish with the flaked almonds. Serve immediately, accompanied with fresh garden vegetables.

SERVES 4

1 × 2 kg/4½ lb boiling chicken
1 carrot, peeled and chopped
1 onion, peeled
1 bayleaf
8 peppercorns
4 cloves
40 g/1½ oz butter
40 g/1½ oz plain (all purpose) flour
¼ cup/60 ml/4 tbsp horseradish relish
¼ cup/50 g/2 oz blanched almonds, coarsely chopped
15 ml/1 tbsp chopped fresh parsley
⅓ cup/90 ml/6 tbsp fromage frais
salt and freshly ground black pepper
25 g/1 oz flaked almonds, to garnish

SERVES 4 TO 6

8 to 12 chicken drumsticks
30 ml/2 tbsp vegetable oil
1 small onion, chopped
1 carrot, cut into small julienne strips
(see Glossary, page 93)
1 sweet green (bell) pepper, seeded and diced
1 small can pineapple slices in natural juice
(approx. 200 g/7 oz)
30 ml/2 tbsp clear honey
10 ml/2 tsp Worcestershire sauce
30 ml/2 tbsp tomato ketchup
15 ml/1 tbsp mango chutney
30 ml/2 tbsp red wine vinegar
15 ml/1 tbsp cornflour (cornstarch)
2.5 ml/½ level teaspoon salt

Oven temperature: 200 °C/400 °F/Gas 6

SWEET AND SOUR CHICKEN DRUMSTICKS

Sweet and sour dishes have long remained a firm favourite. Although any joint of chicken can be used, the dark meat has always proved most popular. Serve the dish with plain boiled rice.

☐ Heat the oil in a pan and sauté the chicken drumsticks until browned. Remove to one side.

☐ Add the onion and cook until softened. Stir in carrots and cook for a further 3 minutes. Stir in the sweet green (bell) pepper.

☐ Strain the pineapple juice into a measuring jug, and make up to 1¼ cups/300 ml/½ pt with cold water. Chop the pineapple roughly and add to the pan together with the juice.

☐ Stir in the honey, Worcestershire sauce, tomato ketchup and chutney.

☐ Blend together the vinegar and cornflour (cornstarch). Add to the pan with the salt. Bring to the boil stirring, cook for 1 minute.

☐ Pour the sauce into a shallow (approx. 5 cups/2 pt) ovenproof dish. Arrange the drumsticks on top. Cover and cook for 20 minutes.

☐ Remove the cover and cook for a further 15 minutes.

☐ Serve the drumsticks with a little sauce. Pass the remaining sauce separately.

SKEWERED CHICKEN

A healthy and nutritious way of serving chicken to children. Delicious hot with rice or jacket potatoes, or cold as part of a packed lunch.

- ☐ Skin and cut the chicken breasts into small, even-sized cubes (approx. 2 cm/¾ in). Thread them onto 8 small wooden kebab skewers, which have been soaked for ½ hour to stop them burning.
- ☐ Mix together the peanut butter, yogurt, orange rind and black pepper to taste. Spoon the mixture evenly over the skewered chicken. Cover loosely and chill for 4 hours.
- ☐ Arrange the skewers on the rack of the grill (broiler) pan, and spoon over any remaining marinade. Grill (broil) for 4 minutes under a moderate heat. Turn the skewers and grill (broil) for a further 3 minutes.
- ☐ Mix the orange juice with the honey and spoon over the kebabs. Return to the grill (broiler) for a further 2 minutes.
- ☐ Serve hot or cold, garnished with orange segments and watercress.

SERVES 4

3 boneless chicken breasts (approx. 175 g/6 oz each)
30 ml/2 tbsp smooth peanut butter
30 ml/2 tbsp low fat natural yogurt
freshly ground black pepper
grated rind ½ orange
juice 1 orange
15 ml/1 tbsp clear honey

GARNISH
peeled orange segments
sprigs of watercress

SERVES 4

30 ml/2 tbsp olive oil
8 shallots or pickling onions, peeled
seasoned flour
4 part-boned chicken breasts
(approx. 200 g/7 oz each)
1 ¼ cup/300 ml/½ pt chicken stock (broth)
15 ml/1 tbsp Dijon mustard
5 ml/1 tsp fresh thyme
2 cups/250 g/8 oz tiny button mushrooms, wiped
salt and freshly ground black pepper
fresh thyme sprigs to garnish

DIJON CHICKEN WITH MUSHROOMS

Very quick to prepare for the unexpected guest. Although Dijon mustard is used in this recipe, try experimenting with wholegrain or one of the speciality mustards.

☐ Heat the oil in a saucepan, add the shallots or onions and sauté until golden brown.
☐ Skin the chicken breasts and dust lightly with the seasoned flour. Add to the pan and sauté until golden brown all over.
☐ Add the chicken stock (broth), mustard, thyme and salt and pepper to taste. Cover and simmer for 15 minutes.
☐ Add the mushrooms and continue simmering, uncovered, for a further 15 minutes.
☐ Serve immediately, garnished with sprigs of fresh thyme.

SERVES 4

4 chicken legs or breasts (approx. 175 g/6 oz each)
8 sprigs thyme
4 rashers lean bacon, derinded
15 ml/1 tbsp vegetable oil
1 large onion, chopped
2 cloves garlic, finely chopped
8 tomatoes, skinned, deseeded and shredded
5 ml/1 tsp tomato purée (paste)
5 ml/1 tsp plain (all purpose) flour
1 ¼ cups/300 ml/½ pt dry white wine
salt and freshly ground black pepper

GARNISH

8 × 1 cm/½ in slices French bread, toasted
30 ml/2 tbsp parsley, freshly chopped

CHICKEN PROVENCAL

Tomatoes, thyme and garlic provide a taste of Provence. Omit the bacon rashers, if you wish – but you may need to add extra oil. Add the thyme sprigs directly to the pan. Delicious with plain potatoes and green (string or snap) beans.

☐ Skin the chicken joints. Lay a sprig of thyme on the top and underside of each joint and wrap a piece of bacon around it, securing with a cocktail stick.
☐ Heat the oil in a pan and sauté the chicken until the joints and bacon are a deep golden colour. Remove and put to one side.
☐ Add the onion and garlic to the pan and cook until softened. Stir in the tomatoes and purée (paste) and cook for a further minute.
☐ Sprinkle the flour over the onion mixture and stir well until blended. Gradually pour in the wine. Bring to the boil, stirring, until slightly thickened. Reduce heat. Season to taste.
☐ Return the chicken joints to the pan, cover, and simmer for 45 minutes or until the chicken is tender.
☐ Transfer the chicken to a warm serving dish (remove the cocktail sticks). Bring the sauce to the boil and let it bubble until it is reduced to the consistency of single (light) cream.
☐ Pour the sauce over the chicken. Garnish with freshly toasted French bread and a generous sprinkling of the chopped parsley.

Dijon Chicken with Mushrooms

SERVES 4

4 medium sized potatoes
2 large carrots, peeled and chopped
3 sticks celery, chopped
175 g/6 oz shredded green cabbage
4 chicken legs (approx. 175 g/6 oz each)
¼ cup/25 g/1 oz seasoned flour
30 ml/2 tbsp vegetable oil
15 ml/1 tbsp fresh thyme, chopped
salt and freshly ground black pepper
1 ¼ cups/300 ml/½ pt beef stock (broth)
⅔ cup/150 ml/¼ pt Guinness or stout
15 ml/1 tbsp dark soft brown sugar
1 egg, beaten
chopped fresh thyme, to garnish

Oven temperature: 180 °C/350 °F/Gas 4

COUNTRY CHICKEN HOTPOT

Reminiscent of the Irish hot pot, made even more authentic by the addition of some Irish stout!

☐ Peel the potatoes; cut two of the potatoes into thin slices, and chop the other two.
☐ Mix the chopped potato with the carrot, celery and cabbage.
☐ Dust the chicken legs with seasoned flour. Heat the oil in a large pan and sauté the chicken legs until lightly golden on all sides. Add the thyme, and salt and pepper to taste.
☐ Place half of the mixed vegetables in the base of a deep casserole. Top with the chicken legs and then the remaining vegetables.
☐ Mix the stock (broth), Guinness or stout and brown sugar together and pour over the contents of the casserole.
☐ Overlap the potato slices in concentric circles on top of the vegetables and chicken. Brush with a little oil.
☐ Cover with a piece of lightly oiled foil and cook for 1 hour.
☐ Remove the foil. Brush the potato crust with the beaten egg. Return to the oven for a further 35 to 40 minutes. Serve sprinkled with chopped thyme.

ROAST CHICKEN WITH WALNUT AND PEAR STUFFING

Pears are often neglected in savoury cooking, but here they prove their worth in a delicious nutty stuffing.

- ☐ Mix the chopped pear with the breadcrumbs, walnuts, ginger and salt and pepper to taste. Mix in the egg yolk to bind the stuffing together.
- ☐ Push the cloves into the skin of the half lemon and place inside the chicken.
- ☐ Press the pear stuffing into the neck cavity of the chicken and fold the remaining neck skin neatly underneath the bird, to secure the stuffing.
- ☐ Place the chicken in a roasting dish, season with salt and pepper, and brush all over with honey. Cook in a preheated oven for 1¼–1½ hours. Baste several times during cooking, spooning the honeyed juices over the chicken.
- ☐ To prepare the glazed pears for the garnish, gently heat together the pear slices and the honey in the pan, turning the pears from time to time until they become translucent.
- ☐ To serve, carve or joint the bird and serve accompanied with some stuffing and a few glazed pear slices.

SPICED SPATCHOCK

Although spatchcock refers generally to a roasting chicken, poussins (Cornish game hens) are just as good and more convenient to prepare and serve. If they are barbecued, baste them with any remaining marinade and a little olive oil. Serve with a salad and potatoes boulangère.

- ☐ Split the birds in half by cutting down one side of the backbone. Open the birds out and turn them over.
- ☐ Rub the poussins (Cornish game gens) with the lemon juice and olive oil. Place in a shallow heatproof dish.
- ☐ In a bowl, mix together the lemon rind, shallot, garlic, peppercorns, coriander, juniper berries and allspice. Press the mixture over the birds.
- ☐ Tuck small pieces of rosemary in around the wing and leg joints.
- ☐ Cover and leave to stand for 2 hours or refrigerate for 8 hours or overnight.
- ☐ Sprinkle the poussins (Cornish game hens) with a little Tabasco and cook under a hot grill (broiler) for 20 to 30 minutes, turning and basting occasionally with the juices.
- ☐ Serve, with any remaining pan juices, garnished with sprigs of fresh rosemary.

SERVES 6

1 small ripe pear, peeled, cored and chopped
1 cup/50 g/2 oz fresh wholemeal breadcrumbs
25 g/1 oz chopped walnuts
generous pinch ground ginger
salt and freshly ground black pepper
1 egg yolk
5 cloves
½ lemon
1 × 1.5 kg/3½ lb oven-ready chicken
30 ml/2 tbsp clear honey
GARNISH
1 pear, cored and sliced
15 ml/1 tbsp clear honey

Oven temperature: 200 °C/400 °F/Gas 6

SERVES 2

2 poussins (Cornish game hens),
approx. 500 g/1 lb each
grated rind and juice 1 small lemon
15 ml/1 tbsp olive oil
1 shallot or small sweet onion, finely chopped
1 clove garlic, finely chopped
10 ml/2 tsp green peppercorns, crushed
5 ml/1 tsp coriander (cilantro) seeds, crushed
4 juniper berries, crushed
2.5 ml/½ tsp ground allspice
2 sprigs rosemary, plus extra for garnish
dash Tabasco

SERVES 6

1 × 1.5 kg/3½ lb oven-ready chicken
sprigs of fresh herbs
wedge of lemon
salt and freshly ground black pepper
¼ cup/60 ml/4 tbsp vegetable oil
2 medium onions, sliced
1 large clove garlic, chopped
1 aubergine (eggplant), cubed
3 medium potatoes, cubed
125 g/4 oz green (string or snap) beans
1 sweet red (bell) pepper, deseeded and sliced
1 sweet green (bell) pepper, deseeded and sliced
175 g/6 oz courgettes (zucchini) cut into chunks
½ cup/125 g/4 oz button mushrooms
5 cups/1.2 1/2 pt chicken stock (broth)

GARNISH

30 ml/2 tbsp chopped walnuts
15 ml/1 tbsp chopped fresh herbs

GARDEN CHICKEN

A wholesome 'hot pot' with an abundance of fresh vegetables. Accompany with wholemeal pasta, such as tagliatelle.

□ Open up the cavity of the chicken and put the sprigs of herbs and the lemon in the centre. Season inside and out with salt and pepper. Place the chicken in a large pan or flameproof casserole.

□ Heat the oil in a pan; add the onion and garlic and cook gently for 2 to 3 minutes. Add the aubergine (eggplant) and cook for a further 3 minutes. Add these to the chicken together with the remaining vegetables and the stock (broth).

□ Bring to the boil and simmer the chicken and vegetables gently in a covered pan for 1½ hours.

□ Sprinkle with the nuts and chopped herbs and serve either straight from the casserole, or lift the chicken out onto a serving dish and surround with the cooked vegetables.

NOTE

If you like really crunchy vegetables then cook the chicken in the stock (broth) with the aubergine (eggplant) and add remaining vegetables during the last 30 minutes cooking time.

POULET AU POT

Chicken in the pot! It was Henry IV's wish that every family in his kingdom should be able to afford and enjoy this simple, but excellent, example of French cooking every Sunday. Hundreds of years later, it is still the perfect, trouble-free meal for all the family. Serve it with saffron rice or creamed potatoes.

☐ Place the chicken and bacon in a large pan or casserole and gently sauté them in their own fat, until tinged brown. Remove the chicken.

☐ Stud 2 of the onions with the cloves and add these to the pan, together with the remaining onions, garlic, carrot chunks and celery. Cover and 'sweat' over a gentle heat for 5 minutes.

☐ Return the chicken to the pan. Pour on the wine and stock (broth), add the bouquet garni and season well.

☐ Very slowly bring to the simmer, skim and cook gently until the chicken is very tender. This may take 1½–2 hours. (The longer and slower it cooks, the better the end result.)

☐ Add the whole button mushrooms 30 minutes before the end.

☐ When done, remove the chicken, vegetables and bacon to a warm serving dish. Strain a scant 2 cups/450 ml/¾ pt of the stock (broth) into a measuring jug (reserve the remainder for other use). Degrease the stock at this stage.

☐ Return the measured stock and milk to the saucepan. Add the lemon juice. Boil the liquid fiercely to reduce it a little.

☐ Meanwhile, prepare the 'beurre manié' – cream the butter and flour together to form a smooth paste. Whisk in the paste, a little at a time, until the sauce thickens. Simmer for 3 to 4 minutes. Check the seasonings.

☐ Serve the chicken whole coated with some of the sauce and surrounded with the bacon and vegetables. Carve the chicken at the table, serving the remainder of the sauce separately.

SERVES 4 TO 6

1 × 1.75 kg/4 lb oven-ready chicken, with giblets
250 g/8 oz piece streaky bacon, derinded and cubed
8 button onions
2 cloves
1 clove garlic, crushed (minced)
2 large carrots, cut into 2.5 cm/1 inch chunks
1 stick celery, sliced
⅔ cup/150 ml/¼ pt dry white wine
10 cups/2 1/4 pt chicken stock (made with the giblets, see page 11)
bouquet garni made up of 1 small bunch parsley stalks, 1 bayleaf, and 2 sprigs of fresh thyme
salt and freshly ground black pepper
⅔ cup/150 ml/¼ pt milk
250 g/½ lb button mushrooms
squeeze lemon juice
15 ml/1 heaped tbsp butter
15 ml/1 heaped tbsp flour

ELIZABETH FRINK'S ROAST LEMON CHICKEN

If you are wanting a plain roast chicken, perhaps to joint and eat cold, or to carve and enjoy without any trimmings, try this recipe. Serve it with baby new potatoes and ratatouille or an aubergine (eggplant) and tomato casserole.

☐ Rub the outside of the chicken with the grated rind of 1 lemon. Chop up the remainder of the lemon and tuck inside the chicken cavity, with the garlic clove.

☐ Season, place in a roasting tray. Pour the olive oil over the chicken, and place the butter inside the cavity. Roast for 1½ hours.

☐ Half an hour before the end of cooking, remove the chicken from the oven, squeeze the juice of the other lemon over it and sprinkle with the chopped parsley.

☐ Cook for the remaining ½ hour. Serve hot or cold.

NOTE

The cooking juices can be skimmed and used in a sauce or gravy if required, or reduced (*see Glossary, page 94*) with a little white wine and simply poured over the carved chicken.

SERVES 4

1 × 1.5 kg/ 3 lb oven-ready chicken
2 lemons
1 clove garlic. peeled
salt and freshly ground black pepper
30 ml/2 tbsp olive oil
2 tbsp/25 g/1 oz butter
30 ml/2 tbsp chopped fresh parsley

Oven temperature: 170 °C/325 °F/Gas 3

SERVES 4

FRESH TOMATO SAUCE
1 onion, finely chopped
2 cloves garlic, finely chopped
30 ml/2 tbsp olive oil
1 kg/2 lb ripe tomatoes, roughly chopped
15 ml/1 tbsp chopped parsley
15 ml/1 tbsp chopped basil
2 sprigs fresh thyme
10 ml/2 tsp caster (fine) sugar
salt and freshly ground black pepper

STUFFING
15 ml/1 tbsp olive oil
1 onion, finely chopped
½ sweet red (bell) pepper, finely chopped
250 g/8 oz courgette (zucchini), grated
25 g/1 oz pinenuts, toasted
2 cups/125 g/4 oz fresh breadcrumbs
15 ml/1 tbsp freshly grated Parmesan cheese
5 ml/1 tsp French mustard
45 ml/3 tbsp freshly chopped chervil
15 ml/1 tbsp freshly chopped tarragon
salt and freshly ground black pepper

2 poussins (Cornish game hens),
(approx. 500 g/1 lb each)
15 ml/1 tbsp olive oil
¼ cup/50 g/2 oz dry breadcrumbs
(preferably home made)
2.5 ml/½ tsp mustard powder

Oven temperature: 180 °C/350 °F/Gas 4

COURGETTE (ZUCCHINI) STUFFED POUSSIN (CORNISH GAME HEN)

Because there is a stuffing and a sauce to accompany the poussin (Cornish game hen), you will find that one bird between two people is quite sufficient. Serve with fresh vegetables.

☐ First make the sauce. Sauté the onion and garlic in the olive oil until golden and softened. Add the remaining ingredients and approximately 1¼ cups/300 ml/½ pt water. Cover and simmer gently for 35 to 40 minutes. Push the sauce through a fine sieve and return to the rinsed pan. If you require a thicker sauce, boil rapidly at this stage to reduce slightly. Adjust seasoning and reheat to serve.

☐ For the stuffing, heat the oil in a pan and add the onion, sweet red (bell) pepper and courgette. Cover and 'sweat' for 2 to 3 minutes or until softened.

☐ Remove from the heat, stir in the pinenuts, breadcrumbs, cheese, fresh mustard, herbs and seasoning to taste.

☐ Rub the surface of the poussin with some olive oil. Sprinkle a mixture of the dry breadcrumbs and mustard over the poussins (Cornish game hens) and lightly press in.

☐ Press the stuffing into the interior of each poussin (Cornish game hen) half. Cover with a small square of foil just large enough to form a lip around the poussin. Gently turn the poussins upright onto a baking tray.

☐ Cook for 30 to 40 minutes or until tender and crisp on the surface.

☐ Serve accompanied with the Fresh Tomato Sauce.

SPECIAL OCCASIONS & ENTERTAINING

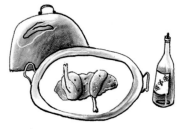

BRAISED CHICKEN IN WHITE WINE WITH TOMATO AND RICE STUFFING

Nutty brown rice is used in the stuffing to make this a perfect dinner party recipe. Serve the sauce separately for those who want to control the flow of calories.

☐ Prepare the stuffing by mixing together the rice, garlic sausage, parsley, tomatoes and 1 egg yolk. Season with salt and pepper. Spoon inside the neck end of the chicken and fold the flap of skin over (securing with a small metal skewer if necessary).

☐ Place the sweet red (bell) pepper under a hot grill (broiler), and turn until it is blistered all over. Put in a polythene bag and leave to 'sweat' for 10 minutes. The skin can then easily be removed. Discard the seeds and thickly slice the flesh.

☐ Heat the oil in a large flameproof casserole, add the chicken and cook over a moderate heat, turning until golden brown all over. Lift out and set aside; add the shallots or onion and mushrooms to the pan and cook for a few minutes until softened.

☐ Return the chicken to the casserole, add the sliced sweet (bell) pepper and pour over the wine and stock. Cover and cook in the oven for 1 hour 20 minutes, or until tender.

☐ Lift the chicken out onto a serving dish and remove the skewer if necessary. Using a slotted spoon, arrange the mushrooms and peppers around the chicken, and keep warm.

☐ Stir the basil into the pan and simmer on the hob for 5 minutes. Beat the remaining egg yolk, cornflour (cornstarch) and cream together and stir into the pan. Heat gently until the sauce thickens.

☐ Joint or carve the chicken and accompany each serving with a spoonful of stuffing. Serve the sauce separately.

SERVES 6

125 g/4 oz cooked brown rice
75 g/3 oz garlic sausage, chopped
15 ml/1 tbsp fresh parsley, chopped
3 tomatoes, skinned, deseeded and chopped
salt and freshly ground black pepper
2 egg yolks
1 × 1.5 kg/3½ lb oven-ready chicken
1 sweet red (bell) pepper
30 ml/2 tbsp olive oil
1 shallot or small sweet onion, finely chopped
125 g/4 oz large cup mushrooms, thickly sliced
1¼ cups/300 ml/½ pt chicken stock (broth)
10 ml/2 tsp cornflour (cornstarch)
45 ml/3 tbsp single (light) cream
10 ml/2 tsp freshly chopped basil (½ tsp dried)

Oven temperature: 180 °C/350 °F/Gas 4

SERVES 4

4 boneless chicken breasts (approx. 150 g/5 oz each), skinned
15 ml/1 tbsp seasoned plain (all purpose) flour
2 tbsp/25 g/1 oz butter
15 ml/1 tbsp light olive oil
¼ cup/60 ml/4 tbsp Calvados (optional)
1 ¼ cups/300 ml/½ pt medium cider
⅔ cup/150 ml/¼ pt fromage frais or single (light) cream
30 ml/2 tbsp hazelnuts, coarsely chopped
GARNISH
2 dessert apples, preferably Cox's
15 ml/1 tbsp lemon juice
15 ml/1 tbsp butter

CHICKEN NORMANDY WITH HAZELNUTS

This is definitely a recipe for that special occasion. The delicious combination of chicken in a creamy cider sauce, apples and hazelnuts, needs only fresh garden vegetables to set it off.

- ☐ Split the chicken breasts, but not all the way through, and open out and flatten to form a neat 'butterfly' shape. Dust with the flour.
- ☐ Heat the butter and oil in a pan and brown the breasts on each side.
- ☐ If using the Calvados heat it in a small pan or ladle, ignite with a match and pour, flaming, onto the chicken. Pour in the cider, cover and simmer until the breasts are tender and cooked. Remove and keep warm.
- ☐ While the chicken is simmering, cut the unpeeled apples into wedges or thick slices. Remove the cores and toss in lemon juice. Sauté the apple in the butter until heated through but still firm.
- ☐ Boil the cooking liquid to reduce by half. Taste and adjust seasonings. Stir in fromage frais or cream and hazelnuts. Gently reheat.
- ☐ Serve each chicken breast with some sauce spooned over it and the remainder passed round separately. Garnish with the apple wedges or slices. Serve immediately.

SERVES 4

1 x 1.25 kg/3 lb oven-ready chicken
15 ml/1 tbsp vegetable oil
1 cup/125 g/4 oz button mushrooms, halved
2 shallots or 1 small sweet onion, finely chopped
15 g/½ oz plain (all purpose) flour
30 ml/2 tbsp brandy
½ cup/125 ml/4 fl oz dry white wine
10 ml/2 tsp tomato purée (paste)
1 ¼ cups/300 ml/½ pt chicken stock (broth)
5 ml/1 tsp chopped fresh tarragon
5 ml/1 tsp chopped fresh chervil
salt and freshly ground black pepper
GARNISH
freshly chopped parsley
4 heart-shaped toasted bread croûtes (see Glossary, page 93)

CHICKEN CHASSEUR

Any recipe which has 'Chasseur' in its title will almost certainly include mushrooms, shallots and white wine in the list of ingredients. This special chicken dish is easy to prepare, can be made in advance and reheated successfully. Accompany with fresh vegetables.

- ☐ Joint the chicken into 8 pieces (*see page 10*).
- ☐ Heat the oil in a large pan and cook the chicken leg joints gently for 5 to 6 minutes, turning once. Then add the wings and breast and sauté slowly until golden brown all over. Remove, cover and keep warm.
- ☐ Add the shallots or onion to the pan and cook for 1 to 2 minutes or until softened and golden. Stir in the mushrooms and continue to cook until they become golden. (Add a little more oil if necessary.)
- ☐ Sprinkle on the flour and blend into the mixture. Gradually stir in the brandy, wine and tomato purée (paste) and stock (broth), until the mixture is smooth and thickened. Season to taste.
- ☐ Return the chicken joints to the pan. Sprinkle in the tarragon and chervil and simmer, half covered, for 10 to 15 minutes.
- ☐ Serve, garnished with the croûtes and a sprinkling of parsley.

CHICKEN AND APPLE PARCELS WITH CALABRESE

- ☐ Place each chicken breast between a sheet of greaseproof paper and flatten with a rolling pin.
- ☐ Peel, core and slice one apple. Divide the slices between the centres of each chicken breast and roll up. Wrap each breast with 2 rashers bacon, securing with wooden cocktail sticks to make 4 neat parcels.
- ☐ Heat the oil and garlic in a pan, and add the chicken parcels. Cook gently for 10 minutes, browning on all sides.
- ☐ Peel and core the remaining apple and cut across to form rings. Place one ring on top of each parcel, add the apple juice. Cover and simmer gently for 15 minutes.
- ☐ Cook the calabrese in boiling salted water for 10 minutes or until tender.
- ☐ Meanwhile, melt the butter in a large frying pan, add the almonds and cook gently, stirring continuously, until browned.
- ☐ Drain the calabrese, transfer to a warm serving dish and sprinkle with the almonds.
- ☐ Remove the chicken to a warm serving dish. Blend the cornflour with the water and add to the pan juices. Stir and cook until thickened. Spoon the sauce over each parcel and garnish with chopped parsley. Serve the calabrese separately.

SERVES 4

4 boneless chicken breasts (each approx. 200 g/7 oz), skinned
2 crisp eating apples
8 rashers smoked bacon, derinded
15 ml/1 tbsp sunflower oil
1 clove garlic, crushed (minced)
1 ¼ cups/300 ml/½ pt apple juice (preferably English)
750 g/1 ½ lb calabrese or broccoli, washed and trimmed
2 tbsp/25 g/1 oz butter
¼ cup/50 g/2 oz flaked almonds
5 ml/1 tsp cornflour (cornstarch)
15 ml/1 tbsp water
salt and freshly ground black pepper
parsley, freshly chopped

SERVES 4

½ cup/125 g/4 oz unsalted butter
grated rind ½ lemon
5 ml/1 tsp lemon juice
1 clove garlic, finely chopped
30 ml/2 tbsp freshly chopped parsley or chervil
pinch ground nutmeg
4 boneless chicken breasts (approx. 175 g/6 oz each)

COATING

¼ cup/25 g/1 oz plain (all-purpose) seasoned flour
3 cups/175 g/6 oz fresh white breadcrumbs
1 large egg (size 1), beaten
¼ cup/60 ml/4 tbsp vegetable oil

GARNISH

fresh parsley or chervil

Oven temperature: 190 °C/375 °F/Gas 5

Chicken Kiev

CHICKEN KIEV

Traditionally, this sinful but classic Russian dish used part-boned chicken fillets (filets), but boneless chicken breasts are perhaps more convenient and economical. However, there is no escaping the buttery garlicky filling which oozes calories, so, as a compromise, these kievs are baked in the oven, rather than deep fried.

☐ To make the filling, cream together the first six ingredients. Shape the savoury butter into a rectangle, wrap in foil and chill until hard.

☐ Remove the skins from the chicken. Cut a small pocket in the side of each breast. Gently beat the breasts between 2 sheets of greaseproof paper to flatten slightly.

☐ Cut the hard butter into 4 fingers and tuck each one into a breast pocket. Fold the cut edge over neatly and secure, if necessary, with a cocktail stick.

☐ Dust the chicken with the lighly seasoned flour, then dip in the beaten egg and coat with the breadcrumbs, pressing them on firmly. Refrigerate for an hour.

☐ Place the kievs on a lightly oiled baking tray. Drizzle over the oil and cook for 35 to 45 minutes or until the coating is golden brown and crisp. Serve immediately, garnished with chopped parsley or chervil.

CHICKEN MARENGO

This classic dish dates back to 1800 when, according to legend, Napoleon's chef created this recipe in celebration of their victory at the Battle of Marengo. Ingredients then included freshwater crayfish, substituted in this version with a garnish of cooked prawns (shrimp). Accompany with new potatoes or noodles.

☐ Heat the oil and sauté the chicken portions until golden all over. Add the onions and garlic and continue cooking until the onion softens.

☐ Sprinkle over the flour, and cook, stirring, until the fat is absorbed and the flour turns a deep golden brown.

☐ Gradually blend in the stock and Marsala. Bring to the boil, then reduce the heat to a simmer and cook, covered, for 10 minutes.

☐ Stir in the tomatoes, purée (paste), mushrooms, basil and brandy. Season to taste and simmer, uncovered, for a further 40 minutes. Remove the saucepan lid for the last 20 minutes, to allow the sauce to reduce. Stir occasionally to prevent the sauce sticking.

☐ Serve, garnished with fresh cooked prawns (shrimp) and fresh basil leaves.

SERVES 4

45 ml/3 tbsp olive oil
4 chicken thighs, skinned
4 chicken drumsticks, skinned
1 large onion, chopped
2 cloves garlic, chopped
¼ cup/25 g/1 oz plain (all purpose) flour
⅔ cup/150 ml/¼ pt chicken stock (broth)
1¼ cups/300 ml/½ pt Marsala or medium white wine
6 tomatoes, skinned and chopped
15 ml/1 tbsp tomato purée (paste)
250 g/8 oz button mushrooms, halved
15 ml/1 tbsp chopped fresh basil
15 ml/1 tbsp brandy
salt and freshly ground black pepper

GARNISH

8 cooked prawns (shrimp)
fresh basil leaves

CHICKEN IN CARROT AND SPINACH JACKETS

Remarkably colourful, bursting with flavour and up-to-the-minute with style, this dish is very simple to make.

□ Trim the chicken breasts to give nice even-sized supremes.

□ Boil the carrots for 10 to 15 minutes until 'al dente'. Refresh under cold running water and pat dry. Grate coarsely and mix with the cheese. Season with a little salt, plenty of black pepper and the allspice.

□ Blanch the spinach leaves in rapidly boiling water for a few seconds, then plunge into a bowl of cold water, to refresh. Drain and pat dry.

□ Place each chicken breast on two overlapping spinach leaves, evenly coat the 4 chicken portions with the carrot and cheese mixture, cover with a third leaf and wrap into neat parcels.

□ Put the prepared vegetables (julienne) on the bottom of an ovenproof dish, arrange the chicken parcels on top and pour over the wine.

□ Cover and bake in a preheated oven for 40 to 45 minutes, basting from time to time to prevent the spinach from drying out.

□ To make the sauce, strain off the cooking liquid into a small saucepan. (Keep the chicken and vegetables warm.) Rapidly boil the cooking liquid until it has reduced to a couple of tablespoonfuls. Reduce the heat and gradually whisk in the yogurt or fromage frais, and the mint. Lightly season.

□ Slice the chicken breasts carefully and fan them out over a bed of vegetables julienne. Trickle over a little sauce and serve the remainder separately.

SERVES 4

4 boneless chicken breasts, skinned (150–175 g/5–6 oz each)
500 g/1 lb carrots, peeled
125 g/4 oz curd or ricotta cheese
salt and freshly ground black pepper
2.5 ml/½ tsp ground allspice
12–16 young spinach leaves, depending on size
375 g/12 oz mixed vegetables, such as courgettes (zucchini), leeks, sweet (bell) peppers and mooli cut into julienne strips and blanched (see Glossary, page 93)
⅔ cup/150 ml/5 fl oz dry white wine
⅔ cup/150 ml/5 fl oz low fat yogurt or fromage frais
15 ml/1 tbsp fresh mint, chopped (or 1 tsp dried mint)

Oven temperature: 180 °C/350 °F/Gas 4

SERVES 4

4 part-boned chicken breasts
(approx. 200 g/7 oz each),
50 g/2 oz celery
50 g/2 oz carrots, peeled
50 g/2 oz green (string or snap) beans, top and tailed
⅔ cup/150 ml/¼ pt chicken stock (broth)
I bayleaf
30 ml/2 tbsp white wine
I bunch watercress, trimmed of coarse stalks
2 spring onions (scallions), trimmed and chopped
75 g/3 oz fromage frais
5 ml/I tsp cornflour (cornstarch) blended with
5 ml/I tsp water
salt and freshly ground black pepper

CHICKEN BREAST WITH WATERCRESS SAUCE

This chicken dish looks very fresh and colourful and provides sufficient vegetables to need only the addition of new potatoes when serving. If you have a steamer, cook the chicken over the stock for 25 to 30 minutes. The vegetables can also be steamed briefly.

☐ Skin the chicken breasts and season lightly.

☐ Prepare the vegetables and cut into julienne strips (*see Glossary, page 93*).

☐ In a pan, bring the stock to a steady simmer. Add the chicken and bayleaf and cover with a tight fitting lid.

☐ Cook gently for 35 to 40 minutes or until the chicken is tender.

☐ Transfer the chicken to a warm serving plate. Add the seasoning and the spring onions to the stock. (Remove and discard the bayleaf.) Bring to the boil and rapidly bubble until the stock has reduced a little.

☐ Add the white wine and the watercress, reserving a few leaves for the garnish. Remove the heat and allow to stand for one minute for the watercress to wilt.

☐ Meanwhile, cook the vegetable julienne in boiling water until just 'al dente' – no more than 5 minutes. Drain and keep warm.

☐ Strain the stock into a measuring jug. Transfer the watercress and spring onions (scallions) to a food processor or blender and add ⅓ cup/90 ml/6 tbsp stock, the fromage frais and the blended cornflour (cornstarch). Purée to a smooth sauce. Season to taste.

☐ Reheat gently, stirring, until thickened. Adjust the consistency of the sauce with a little more stock if desired.

☐ To serve, place each chicken breast on a plate. Spoon over the vegetables julienne and pour the watercress sauce around the chicken. Garnish with the reserved watercress leaves.

CHICKEN IN SWEET RED (BELL) PEPPER AND ALMOND SAUCE

A colourful chicken dish, enhanced with a nutty, spicy flavour that requires little accompaniment other than plain boiled rice to help mop up the juices.

☐ Skin the chicken breasts and cut into pieces approximately 4 cm × 1 cm (2 in × ½ in). Heat a third of the oil in a pan and cook the chicken for 5 minutes. Drain and transfer to a plate.

☐ Combine the onion, ginger, garlic, almonds, sweet red (bell) peppers, cumin, coriander, turmeric, cayenne and salt in a food processor or liquidizer. Blend to a smooth paste.

☐ Heat the remaining oil. Add the paste and cook for 10 to 12 minutes, stirring occasionally. Add the chicken pieces, water, star anise, lemon juice and black pepper to taste. Cover, reduce the heat and simmer gently for 25 minutes or until the chicken is tender. Stir once or twice during cooking.

SERVES 4

4 boneless chicken breasts, (approx. 175/6 oz each)
⅓ cup/90 ml/6 tbsp sunflower oil
I medium onion, roughly chopped
2 cm/I in fresh ginger, peeled
3 cloves garlic
25 g/I oz blanched almonds
375 g/12 oz sweet red (bell) pepper, deseeded and chopped
15 ml/I tbsp ground cumin
10 ml/2 tsp ground coriander (cilantro)
5 ml/I tsp turmeric
pinch Cayenne pepper
2.5 ml/½ tsp salt
⅔ cup/150 ml/¼ pt water
3 whole star anise (a Chinese spice)
30 ml/2 tbsp lemon juice
freshly ground black pepper

Chicken in Sweet Red (Bell) Pepper and Almond Sauce

CHICKEN A LA KING

This dish can be made a day or two in advance and kept covered in the refrigerator until required. Serve with plain boiled rice, to help mop up the juices.

☐ Skin the chicken breasts and cut into bite-size pieces.

☐ Heat the butter and half the oil in a large frying pan. Add the mushrooms and sweet (bell) peppers and stir-fry until the peppers are just turning tender. Transfer, with a slotted spoon, onto absorbent kitchen paper (paper towel), to drain.

☐ Add the remaining oil to the pan and add the chicken pieces in a single layer. Sauté until golden brown. Season with salt and pepper.

☐ Stir in the stock, fromage frais and the brandy and cornflour (cornstarch), blended together. Continue to stir, over a low heat, until the sauce begins to thicken. Gently simmer, uncovered, for 5 minutes. Check seasoning and adjust if necessary.

☐ Stir in the mushrooms and sweet (bell) peppers and cook for a further 3 to 4 minutes. Serve on a bed of rice, garnished with fresh watercress.

SERVES 6

6 boneless chicken breasts (approx. 150 g/5 oz each)
2 tbsp/25 g/I oz butter
30 ml/2 tbsp vegetable oil
300 g/10 oz button mushrooms, thickly sliced
I sweet red (bell) pepper, deseeded and cut into 2.5 cm/I in squares
I sweet yellow (bell) pepper, deseeded and cut into 2.5 cm/I in squares
I sweet green (bell) pepper, deseeded and cut into 2.5 cm/I in squares
few strands saffron, soaked in 30 ml/2 tbsp boiling water
⅔ cup/150 ml/¼ pt chicken stock (broth)
I ¼ cups/300 ml/½ pt fromage frais or low fat yogurt
30 ml/2 tbsp brandy or medium sherry
10 ml/2 tsp cornflour (cornstarch)
salt and freshly ground black pepper
fresh watercress, to garnish

SERVES 4

*4 boneless chicken breasts
(approx. 175 g/6 oz each),*

MARINADE

*⅔ cup/150 ml/¼ pt white wine
¼ cup/60 ml/4 tbsp Pernod
juice of 1 large lemon
15 ml/1 tbsp olive oil
5 ml/1 tsp crushed black peppercorns
pinch dill weed
pinch sea salt*

STUFFING

*½ cup/125 g/4 oz low fat cream cheese
12 peeled prawns (shrimp), chopped
5 ml/1 tsp chopped parsley
2.5 ml/½ tsp fennel seeds
salt and freshly ground black pepper*

GARNISH

sprigs fresh fennel or dill

Oven temperature: 190 °C/375 °F/Gas 5

WOODS' MARINATED CHICKEN WITH PRAWN (SHRIMP) AND FENNEL

Long marinating is the secret to the success of this recipe. It is essential to allow the chicken flavours to fully develop. Start preparing this dish a day in advance.

☐ Lay the chicken breasts in a shallow dish. Pour over the marinade ingredients. Cover and chill for 24 hours.

☐ Remove chicken breasts and reserve the marinade.

☐ Beat together the stuffing ingredients. Make a deep incision in the side of each chicken breast, and spoon the stuffing mixture into the pocket. Secure the edges with a cocktail stick. Transfer to a shallow roasting dish.

☐ Cook for 25 minutes or until the chicken is tender. Carefully remove and discard the chicken skin and cocktail sticks. Transfer the chicken to a warm serving plate.

☐ Deglaze the juices in the roasting dish with the reserved marinade. Place over a high heat and boil the marinade until it has reduced slightly. Check seasoning. Pour over the chicken.

☐ Garnish with sprigs of fresh dill or fennel, and accompany with fresh garden vegetables.

CHICKEN ARDENNAISE

SERVES 4

750 g/1 ½ lb boneless chicken breast
2 thick gammon rashers (smoked raw ham)
(125 g/4 oz each)
1 cup/250 ml/8 fl oz white wine
3 shallots or small sweet onions, finely chopped
salt and freshly ground black pepper
30 ml/2 tbsp plain (all purpose) flour
2 tbsp/25 g/1 oz butter
15 ml/1 tbsp vegetable oil
⅔ cup/150 ml/¼ pt fromage frais
10 ml/2 tsp Dijon mustard
15 ml/1 tbsp chopped parsley

This is a good dish for special occasions, but it does need the attention of the cook at the last minute. Serve with rice or new potatoes and fresh garden vegetables.

- ☐ Skin chicken, and cut into bite-size pieces. Put in a bowl to one side.
- ☐ Remove the rind and any fat from the gammon (ham) and cut into julienne strips (see Glossary, page 93).
- ☐ Place gammon (ham) in a bowl, together with the white wine and onions. Mix well, cover, and leave to soak for 30 minutes. Drain, reserving the juice.
- ☐ Lightly season the chicken, and turn in the flour until lightly dusted.
- ☐ Heat together the butter and oil in a large frying pan (skillet). Add the chicken and sauté for 4 to 5 minutes or until golden.
- ☐ Add the gammon (ham) and onions and cook for a further 2 minutes.
- ☐ Pour on the reserved wine and fromage frais and simmer, gently, for a further 4 to 5 minutes.
- ☐ Arrange chicken on a serving dish, cover and keep warm. Reduce the sauce a little over a high heat and stir in the mustard and parsley.
- ☐ Spoon sauce over the chicken and serve immediately.

Chicken Ardennaise

CHICKEN IN CINNAMON AND SAUTERNES SAUCE

SERVES 4

4 boneless chicken breasts (approx. 175g /6 oz each),
skinned
30 ml/2 tbsp sunflower oil
1 medium onion, finely chopped
1 clove garlic, crushed (minced)
7.5 cm/3 in piece of cinnamon stick, bruised
1 ¼ cups/300 ml/½ pt Sauternes (or similar sweet
white wine)
salt and freshly ground black pepper
2 egg yolks
⅔ cup/150 ml/¼ pt low fat natural yogurt or
fromage frais
GARNISH
12 button onions
2 tbsp/25 g/1 oz butter
15 ml/1 tbsp soft brown sugar
crumbled or flaked cinnamon stick
fresh coriander (cilantro)

A new and delicious combination of chicken and cinnamon to grace any dinner party.

- ☐ Heat the oil in a large pan and sauté the chicken breasts until evenly coloured on all sides. Remove and keep warm.
- ☐ Add the onion, garlic and bruised cinnamon stick to the pan and cook for a few minutes or until the onions are softened.
- ☐ Return the chicken to the pan, add the Sauternes and salt and pepper, to taste. Cover and simmer gently for 20 to 25 minutes until the chicken is tender.
- ☐ Meanwhile toss the baby onions in the butter until translucent and well glazed.
- ☐ Transfer the chicken to a serving plate and keep warm. Discard cinnamon stick. Liquidize the cooking juices until smooth. Return to a clean pan.
- ☐ Beat the egg yolks with the yogurt and stir into the sauce. Heat through gently, stirring continuously.
- ☐ Spoon the sauce over the cooked chicken breasts and garnish with the crumbled cinnamon stick, glazed button onions, reheated if necessary and sprigs of fresh coriander (cilantro).

SERVES 4

1 × 1.25/1.75 kg (3½–4 lb) roasting chicken
30 ml/2 tbsp vegetable oil
4 lean bacon rashers, derinded and chopped
12 baby onions or shallots, peeled
2 cloves garlic, chopped
5 cups/1.2 1/2 pt French red table wine
15 ml/1 tsp brandy
15 ml/1 tbsp tomato purée (paste)
2 sprigs fresh thyme
2 bayleaves
2 sprigs fresh parsley
300 g/10 oz small dark-gilled mushrooms
salt and freshly ground black pepper
15 ml/1 tbsp plain (all purpose) flour
15 ml/1 tbsp butter, softened
30 ml/2 tbsp freshly chopped parsley

COQ AU VIN

Originally the French farmer's simple stew using farmhouse chickens and wine from a neighbouring vineyard, this dish is now a classic. As with many casseroles and stews, the flavour will improve if made a day or two in advance.

☐ Joint the chicken into 8 portions (*see page 10*).

☐ Heat the oil in a large, heavy-based pan. Add the chicken in one single layer and sauté until evenly browned all over. Remove from the pan. Drain off all but 15 ml/1 tbsp fat from the pan.

☐ Add the bacon, baby onions or shallots and garlic to the pan and fry until the onions are golden. Stir in the red wine, brandy, tomato purée (paste), fresh herbs and seasoning, to taste.

☐ Return the chicken to the pan. Bring to the boil, then reduce the heat, cover and simmer for 40 minutes. Stir in the mushrooms and simmer, uncovered, for a further 10 minutes. Adjust seasoning, if necessary.

☐ Transfer the chicken, onions and mushrooms to a warm serving plate. Discard the herbs. Bring the sauce to a steady boil and drop in tea-spoonfuls of the creamed flour and butter. (This is called beurre manie.) Whisk continuously, until all the mixture has been added. Simmer for 10 minutes to cook the flour and thicken the sauce.

☐ Pour the sauce over the chicken, then sprinkle with the freshly chopped parsley. Serve immediately, accompanied with fresh vegetables.

CHICKEN AND RICOTTA WITH FRESH TOMATO AND BASIL SAUCE

A very pretty dish, fresh with the vibrant colours of the tomato sauce and spinach filling. Accompany with a salad and new potatoes.

- Flatten each chicken breast, in turn, by beating between 2 pieces of damp greaseproof paper with a rolling pin.
- Remove the spinach leaves from the main stalk and wash well. Shake well, put in a large dry pan and cook until wilted and reduced in volume. Drain, squeezing well to remove excess liquid. Chop finely.
- Mix together the spinach, ricotta, pinenuts and seasoning. Divide the filling between the breasts and spread over each, leaving 1 cm (½ in) gap on one long edge. Roll up each 'roulade' starting with the opposite edge, and secure loosely with strong cotton or fine string. Wrap each breast in a piece of foil and lay in an ovenproof dish.
- Pour in the stock (broth) and poach gently for 30 minutes, or until the chicken is cooked through.
- Meanwhile make the sauce. Chop the tomatoes roughly. Heat the oil and cook gently until softened. Add the tomatoes, purée (paste), sugar and seasoning. Simmer for 30 minutes.
- Liquidize until smooth. Check the seasoning, then stir in the chopped basil. Keep warm until required, then divide between 6 warm plates.
- To serve, remove the chicken, each breast cut into neat slices and arrange on top of the sauce on each plate. Garnish with fresh basil leaves.

SERVES 6

6 boneless chicken breasts, skinned
(approx. 175 g/6 oz each)
500 g/1 lb fresh spinach
175 g/6 oz ricotta cheese
¼ cup/50 g/2 oz pinenuts
salt and freshly ground black pepper
1¼ cups/300 ml/½ pt chicken stock (broth)

SAUCE

500 g/1 lb fresh tomatoes, skinned
15 ml/1 tbsp sunflower oil
1 small onion, diced
15 ml/1 tbsp tomato purée (paste)
5 ml/1 tsp caster (fine) sugar
salt and freshly ground black pepper
30 ml/2 tbsp chopped fresh basil

GARNISH

fresh basil leaves

Oven temperature: 200 °C/400 °F/Gas 6

SERVES 10

2 × 1.25 kg/3 lb chickens
7 cloves garlic
3 large tomatoes
5 ml/1 tsp peppercorns
1 cup/250 ml/8 fl oz red wine vinegar
2 cups/450 ml/15 fl oz chicken stock (broth)
salt and freshly ground black pepper
1 cup/200 g/7 oz fromage frais
45 ml/3 tbsp chopped chives

Chicken Véronique

SERVES 4

4 boneless chicken breasts (approx. 175g/6 oz each),
skinned
1 cup/250 ml/8 fl oz chicken stock (broth)
¼ cup/60 ml/4 tbsp dry white wine
rind and juice ½ lemon
10 ml/2 tsp finely chopped onion
1 bayleaf
sprig tarragon (or pinch dried)
3 peppercorns
10 ml/2 tsp cornflour (cornstarch)
¼ cup/60 ml/4 tbsp fromage frais
salt and white pepper
fresh tarragon, to garnish (optional)

CHICKEN IN VINEGAR SAUCE

This is the perfect dish for a large party, as it is economical, can be made in advance and reheated, and has an enticing sweet-sour aroma. Accompany the dish with fresh noodles or soft creamed potatoes.

☐ Divide each chicken into 10 portions, following the instructions on page 10, plus diagonally halving the breasts. Carefully remove the skin.

☐ Peel and crush the garlic. Skin, deseed and roughly chop the tomatoes.

☐ Heat a large non-stick frying pan; there is no need for any oil. In small batches, brown the chicken portions on all sides for 6 minutes. Remove the chicken pieces and leave to cool on a wire cake rack.

☐ Transfer the chicken to a large casserole. Add garlic, tomatoes and the peppercorns and cook for 1 minute.

☐ Add the vinegar and boil for 3 to 4 minutes to reduce the liquid. Add the stock (broth), cover and simmer for 10 minutes until the chicken is tender.

☐ Remove the chicken from the casserole and allow the pieces to cool again on the wire cake rack.

☐ Bring the liquid in the casserole to the boil again and simmer it gently until it is the consistency of single (cereal) cream. Skim off any fat and froth from time to time.

☐ When there is approximately 2½ cups/600 ml/1 pt sauce, strain it through a fine sieve. Season to taste with pepper and, if required, some salt.

☐ Return the chicken pieces and the sauce to the casserole. The sauce should half cover the chicken.

☐ Gently reheat the casserole. Swirl in the fromage frais and sprinkle with the freshly chopped chives. Serve hot.

CHICKEN VÉRONIQUE

Véronique describes the smooth white wine sauce and sweet green grapes that contribute to this classic dish. Chicken, ham and sole can all be prepared this way. This recipe has been adapted to maintain the sophistication, but lower the calories.

☐ Place the stock, white wine, lemon rind, onion, tarragon, bayleaf and peppercorns in a saucepan. Bring to the boil then reduce the heat to a simmer. Lightly season the chicken breasts and poach them in the liquid for 20 minutes or until tender. (The pan must be covered tightly with a lid.)

☐ Meanwhile, peel and pip (pit) the grapes and toss in the lemon juice. Leave to stand.

☐ Transfer the cooked chicken to a serving dish and keep warm. Strain the stock and return to the saucepan. Boil until reduced by half.

☐ Blend the cornflour with a little cold water (or wine) and stir into the saucepan; continue to boil, stirring, until smooth and thickened. Season to taste.

☐ Remove from the heat and stir in the drained grapes and the fromage frais. Pour the sauce over the chicken and serve immediately, garnished, if you like, with a sprig of fresh tarragon.

GLOSSARY OF USEFUL TERMS

AL DENTE   Italian expression literally meaning 'to the tooth', usually applied to vegetables and pasta to describe the desired texture of the cooked food – firm to the bite, not too soft on the outside and barely cooked at the centre.

BAIN MARIE   A roasting or baking tray half filled with hot water in which terrines, custards etc, stand. The food is protected from the fierce oven heat and cooks in a steamy atmosphere. It also refers to cooking on the hob, using a double boiler or bowl over a saucepan of simmering water – particularly for delicate sauces.

BARDING   A way of protecting lean meat and the breast of dry birds with slices of fat, preferably pork or bacon, before roasting. The fat melts during cooking, thus basting the meat and keeping it moist.

BASTE   To pour or spoon fat or liquid over a food, particularly roast or grilled meats, to prevent it drying out.

BEURRE MANIÉ   Butter and flour mixture used to bind and thicken sauces or soups.

BLANCH   To cook or partly cook a food prior to cooking by another method, such as sweet peppers before stuffing, or potatoes before roasting.
To remove skins from fruits, nuts and certain vegetables by plunging the food into boiling water.

BOUILLON   French term for stocks or broths, from the verb 'bouillir' to boil. Bouillon cubes are well-seasoned stock cubes.

BOUQUET GARNI   A bunch or 'faggot of herbs' used for flavouring and perfuming sauces and stews.

BRAISE·   To cook meat, vegetables, or both, at a low heat in a covered pot, with a little liquid.

BROCHETTE   A French word for skewer, also a dish made by threading meat or other ingredients on a skewer before grilling them.

COULIS   A liquid purée of fruit or vegetables, usually tomatoes, made without flour.

COURT BOUILLON   A seasoned liquid or stock in which to poach fish or shellfish.

CROÛTE   French for crust – a small round or other shape of fried or toasted bread, used to garnish or as a base for a savoury mixture. Croûtons are tiny croûtes.

DEGLAZE   To add liquid (wine or stock for example) to a pan or roasting tin in which food has been fried, sautéed or roasted. The juices and particles on the base are scraped into the liquid and used as a basis for a sauce.

DEGREASE   To skim the fat off liquids such as stocks, soups, sauces and gravies.

DRESS   To pluck, draw (gut) and truss poultry and game.

ESCALOPE   A thin slice of meat, sometimes beaten out flat to make thinner and larger.

FARCE   Another word for a stuffing.

FETA   A Greek curd cheese made from sheeps' milk.

FILLET (FILET)   A prime cut of beef, fish or poultry with all bones removed.

FLAMBÉ   Means 'in flames' and indicates the flaming of brandy or other spirits to burn off the harshness of the alcohol before being used to flavour foods.

FROMAGE FRAIS   French 'fresh cheese'. This is now commercially available and has a light creamy consistency like yogurt. Can replace cream in many recipes.

GARNISH   An edible decoration added to savoury dishes to improve appearance, add variety or colour and awaken the taste buds.

GIBLETS   The liver, heart, gizzard, neck, feet and wingtips of birds. They can be cooked to make a stock, or the edible parts can be cut up and used in stuffings.

GIZZARD   Part of a bird's neck. After being rinsed clean it can be used to make stocks.

GLAZE   To protect, or to improve, the appearance, by adding a gloss. This may be cooking juices from meat, aspic, egg or milk (for pastries) or reduced vegetable juices.

GOUJONS   A French term for small strips of poultry or fish which are generally coated in breadcrumbs for frying.

GRATIN   The French term for a crust, usually made of cheese or breadcrumbs, that is finished off and browned under a hot grill (broiler) or in the oven.

JULIENNE   A French term for food, usually vegetables, cut into matchstick-like strips before being cooked or used as a garnish.

KNEADING   Putting the strength of the whole body behind the hands to work a pastry or dough into a pliable mixture.

LARDING   Threading thin strips of fat (bacon or pork) into very lean joints to make them moist and jucy. A special larding needle is required.

LIAISON   The French term for a thickening agent (egg yolks, flour and/or butter) used for sauces.

MACERATE   To soak fruit in a seasoned liquid so that it absorbs the flavour.

MARINADE   (noun) a seasoning mixture, usually liquid, in which to soak meat, fish, poultry or vegetables to give flavour and to tenderize before cooking. Marinate (verb).

MARSALA   A sweet, dark, fortified wine made from grapes grown in Sicily.

MOZARELLA   Soft kneaded cheese from Italy, traditionally made from buffalos' milk, but now made also from cows' milk.

EN PAPILLOTE   Literally, in an envelope. A wrapping of paper or foil in which fish or meat is baked to retain flavour and aroma.

PARBOIL To partly cook by boiling, prior to completing the cooking by another method.

PILAFF, PILAU In Middle Eastern and Asian cooking, a term for cooked rice.

PINCH A pinch of any dry ingredient is the amount you can pick up between your thumb and finger.

POACH To cook gently in liquid that is usually water, stock or milk. Usually fish and egg dishes. (see Shivering)

POT ROAST To cook meat slowly in a covered pot with little or no added liquid.

PURÉE To work down cooked or soft fruits or vegetables to a smooth thick liquid. This is generally done in a food processor or liquidizer.

QUENELLES A light dumpling mixture of finely minced meat, fish or poultry and egg whites, poached.

REDUCE To boil down a liquid to concentrate its flavour and thicken it to the consistency of a sauce.

REFRESH To plunge hot food into cold water to stop it from cooking further, or to rinse it.

ROUX A mixture of butter and flour used to thicken sauces.

SAUTÉ From the French verb 'to jump' – to fry food in just enough oil to prevent it from sticking.

SEAR To brown meat quickly under a high heat to seal in the juices.

SEASONING Usually refers to salt, pepper and ground spices added to food during cooking.
At the table, they are called 'condiments' from the Latin 'condire', to season or pickle.

SHIVERING A lower temperature than simmering – no bubbles on the surface (82–88 °C/180–190 °F). This is a poaching temperature.

SIMMER To cook in a liquid at just below the boiling point so that the surface of the liquid trembles but bubbles hardly burst. (93–99 °C/200–210°F).

SKIM OR SCUM To remove a frothy, grey/white substance from the surface of a cooking liquid. (It is exuded by meats and vegetables during heating.)

SLAKING Blending a small amount of liquid with a thickening agent such as cornflour or arrowroot, prior to thickening soups, sauces or gravies.

SOY SAUCE A fermented and distilled Chinese sauce, made from soya beans, flour and water.

SPIT-ROAST To roast a joint or fowl on a spit that is turned so the meat is cooked evenly.

STEAMING Cooking by vapour from boiling water, in a well-sealed container.

STIR-FRY To move small pieces of food around constantly in a frying pan or wok, so that they cook rapidly on all sides and do not stick to the pan.

STOCK (BROTH) A base for sauces and stews that is made by simmering giblets and carcass of poultry or meat bones, vegetables and seasoning.

SUPRÊME Choice pieces of poultry or game birds – usually the breast – and fish.

SWEAT To cook vegetables in a little fat over a gentle heat in a covered pan, until they release their juices.

TERRINE A china, earthenware, glass or metal dish used for pâtés, potted meats and desserts. The word also now applies to the food cooked or moulded in the terrine.

TIMBALE A thimble-shaped (but not thimble-sized) mould for the preparation of savoury and sweet mixtures.

TRIVET A metal stand or rack that is placed inside the cooking vessel, usually for roasting joints on, or supporting heatproof basins.

TRUSS To tie a bird or joint of meat with string so that it is compactly arranged for cooking. A trussing needle may be used to thread the string through certain parts of a chicken.

VELOUTÉ A sauce consisting of a roux to which stock has been added.

WILT To cook vegetables such as spinach or lettuce briefly until they soften.

WISHBONE The V-shaped bone in a chicken that links the tip of the breastbone with the shoulder joints.

WOK A large round-bottomed pan used in Chinese cookery.

ZEST The coloured, outer rind of citrus fruits which is scraped or grated off for use in cooking. It contains the essential oils of the fruit.

INDEX OF RECIPES

ACKNOWLEDGEMENTS

To the most aptly named Mr Precious of Thorne Poultry Ltd,
nr Doncaster, Yorkshire, for most generously supplying the
chickens for photography.

Maria Petronijevich of the British Chicken Information Service
for her invaluable assistance, and for the recipes and
photographs on pp. 23, 26 above and below,
29, 30, 31 above, 32, 36 above and below,
37, 38 above and below, 41 below, 42, 43, 46 above,
56, 57, 63 below, 65 above and below, 73 above, 76, 77
above, 78, 83, 84 above, 85, 87 below, 89 below, 91.

James of Shipston-on-Stour, Warwicks.

Hazel Middleton of Kraft General Foods Limited.

The Robert Welch Studio Shop, Chipping Campden, Glos.

Backgrounds Prop Hire, London

Anne, for typing fast and furiously

DEDICATION

For my special godmother
Vera